THE GAME OF WORK

Also by Charles A. Coonradt

Scorekeeping For Success

Managing the Obvious

The Four Laws of Debt Free Prosperity

THE GAME OF WORK

How to Enjoy Work as Much as Play

CHARLES A. COONRADT
with Lee Nelson

Park City, Utah

The Game of Work, LLC, 1912 Sidewinder Drive, Ste. 201,
Park City, Utah 84060, 800-438-6074, email: game@gameofwork.com
www.gameofwork.com

First edition, 1984
Second edition, 1985
Third edition, 1997
Fourth edition, 1999
Fifth edition, 2001

Library of Congress Cataloging-in-Publication Data

Coonradt, Charles A.
    The game of work.

    Includes index.
    1. Employee motivation. 2. Motivation (Psychology)
3. Work—Psychological aspects. I. Nelson, Lee.
II. Title.
HF5549.5.M63C67 1997   658.3'14
ISBN 1-883004-00-4

Printed in the United States of America

10 9 8   7   6   5

To my son Christopher

who taught us about winning
though his game was very short

A portion of the proceeds
from the sale of this book
has been donated
to the Ronald McDonald House
in Christopher's memory

Contents

Foreword

By Paul J. Meyer
Founder and Chairman of the Board
SMI International, Inc.

Over the 25-year history of our company, it has been my privilege to observe hundreds of distributors and sales representatives who have been associated with SMI International, Inc. Many of them have achieved outstanding success and have reached challenging goals both in their personal lives and in building their organizations.

By any set of criteria, Chuck Coonradt belongs among the most successful members of our worldwide organization. Once a distributor for Leadership Management, Inc., a marketing subsidiary of SMI International, Inc., he won recognition as a top personal producer and as the builder of an outstanding and highly successful sales organization. He won virtually every award offered to the sales organization. For five of six consecutive years he was honored as Distributor of the Year for Leadership Management, Inc., an achievement unprecedented in the history of the company. He has also been the recipient of two worldwide awards for outstanding performance.

His ability to work with people in a managerial setting to help them improve productivity and achieve organizational goals and his expertise in communicating from the platform have gained him wide recognition. *The Game of Work* describes many of the techniques he has used to help his LMI clients gain maximum benefits from using the programs produced by our company. The book will provide you with useful ideas and will spark your own creativity as you seek greater success in your organization and in your personal life.

Acknowledgments

No great work is ever accomplished by the writer alone. Just as Plato had Aristotle, the concepts developed in the following pages are based on the efforts, at least in part, of those who have gone before. Napoleon Hill, in his book *Think and Grow Rich*, was the mentor for us all, and my involvement with Success Motivation Institute and its president, Paul J. Meyer, was a springboard for many of the concepts developed in this volume. Since 1971 his programs and tapes have had a profound impact upon my life and accomplishments. I have endeavored in this book to identify specific material borrowed from all sources and wish to express an overall appreciation to the pioneers who made it possible for books like this one to be written.

The testing, modifying, and continuing evolution of this book has been and is being done by all the members of The Game of Work, LLC owe special thanks to our officers and staff, for their ability to put wings on these ideas and make them fly.

Introduction

By Lee Nelson

My first real contact with the main principle discussed in this book occurred one afternoon in 1958 when the manager of the Safeway store I was working for took me into the back room and showed me three four-by-eight-foot wooden bins filled to overflowing with empty pop bottles. I was just beginning my first after-school job.

The manager explained that the bottles needed to be sorted into cases before they could be picked up by the various vendors. He said there were so many bottles in the bins because the adult clerks hated to "work bottles" and avoided the task whenever possible. That was why I was being given the job—as a 16-year-old kid I was at the bottom of the pecking order.

The manager showed me where the empty cases were stored, which bottles could be combined in the same cases, which had to be kept separate, and where the cases of empties needed to be stacked.

Just when I thought I knew all there was to know about the new task and was ready to go to work, the manager said, "It takes most clerks one hour to do a bin. I hope you can do that well."

He looked at his watch. I looked at mine.

"Let me know when you finish the first bin." He turned and walked away.

Suddenly my work took on a new meaning. Working the bottles was not just another job that needed to be done. A standard had been set by which performance would be measured with exactness. The manager was keeping score on me. I was keeping score on myself.

My palms began to sweat. I looked at the bins of bottles with new interest. The manager, like my basketball coach, had put me into a game and turned on the scoreboard. I flew at the bottles.

An hour and ten minutes later I finished the first bin, frustrated at my clumsiness, but confident that if I persisted I could beat the magic 60-minute barrier—the accepted standard in my new working world.

I became the regular bottle worker, and a record was kept on how long it took me to work each bin of bottles. After a month I worked three bins of bottles in one hour—three times the acceptable rate set by my fellow workers. The manager was pleased. The other workers talked about it. I believed I was possibly the fastest bottle worker in the entire Safeway chain. I was proud. Maybe the other workers knew more than I did about checking, cutting meat, or trimming lettuce—but I knew more about working bottles and could do my job twice as fast as anyone else in the store.

The manager of the night stocking crew heard about the kid with the fast hands and arranged for me to be assigned to him as soon as school was out. The night shift worked from 11 p.m. until 8 a.m., and my hourly wage was increased from $1.33 to $2.42 per hour.

Bill Cunningham, the manager of the night crew, was naturally competitive, both on and off the job. Every task was a race to see who was the best and the fastest.

My eyes couldn't follow Bill's price marker as it flew over the cans. He could throw six soup cans at a time onto the shelf, three in each hand, the labels all facing forward when the cans came to rest. On Tuesday nights when we washed and waxed the floors, Bill's mop could perform more tricks than a witch's broom. He learned that in the Navy.

Bill challenged me to try to keep up with him, which

peared an impossible task. But I tried and every week got a little closer. It seemed every task was timed and measured, including the tearing up of boxes for the incinerator. Speed and accuracy were the game, and we kept score. Some of the other night crew members didn't like to race with Bill and me. They thought we were too "gung ho." They seemed to prefer watching the clock instead of beating it.

Nothing felt better than to walk out of that store into the morning sunshine, my body winding down after a night of running full speed in an effort to keep up with or beat Bill. And when Bill would say in parting, "Big load coming in today. Wear your running shoes tonight," it was music to my ears. I felt like an athlete getting ready for the big game.

I went on to finish college, marry, and begin a career in business and writing. In college and future jobs the things I had learned at Safeway didn't seem to apply. There was a difference between beating records and beating people. Being fast wasn't necessarily a desirable quality if you weren't doing the right thing. Sometimes I sensed a lack of direction, even confusion, among my fellow workers. And I was at a loss as to how to apply in different situations the principles that had worked so well at Safeway.

Then I met Chuck Coonradt, a professional businessman, who had taken the principles that had motivated me so effectively at Safeway and applied them to all types of business situations, achieving phenomenal results.

Chuck is the founder of The Game of Work, LLC, a company that teaches executives how to turn business into a game by keeping score. Chuck has figured out how to do for all kinds of businesses what those managers at Safeway did for me. There is no doubt in my mind that Chuck is the world's leading measurement expert.

As a sports enthusiast and former college football player, Chuck has observed that people will pay for the privilege of working harder than they will work for pay. Think about it—we call it recreation.

"In the absence of clearly defined goals, people are forced to concentrate on activity and ultimately become enslaved by it," says Chuck. He continues, "Most businesses pay for attendance when they need to be paying for performance and productivity. Most businesspeople don't keep score, don't measure performance as effectively as they do in recreation."

As Chuck began to tell me about his experiences with many companies, I realized that he was onto something big, something very American, something vital to the success of every business. Chuck has discovered the missing link of all the goal-setting rhetoric of the '60s and '70s. I was amazed at his track record. This stuff really works.

A March of Dimes telethon director developed a simple tracking system, based on dollars raised instead of people contacted—a tracking system that could be updated every hour throughout the telethon, providing continuous feedback. With the new system in place, donations increased from $78,000 to $110,000 in one year. Within three years the telethon went to well over $200,000 a year.

A local beverage distributor began to measure the number of cases delivered per gallons of gas consumed in delivery trucks; he experienced an immediate 22 percent decrease in delivery costs.

A manufacturing firm, within six weeks of introducing a measurement technique in a key manufacturing process, reduced the amount of scrap or wasted material from two bins a day to two bins a week, resulting in an annual savings of over $30,000.

An advertising salesman introduced several of Chuck's measurement techniques and four months later received the largest commission check in his six-year history with the company. He came into The Game of Work program with a goal to increase sales 13 percent, and 90 days later he increased the goal to 47 percent and eventually achieved a 55 percent increase the first year.

A small grocery store improved its shelf-stocking efficiency 33 percent, from 30 to 40 cases per man-hour with the adoption of one simple measuring technique.

A building supply company reduced inventory from

$290,000 to $165,000, freeing $115,000 in operating capital, and at the same time increased the company's ability to fill orders.

A wholesale lumberyard decreased the number of man-hours per invoice from 4 to 1.9 for an annual savings of $147,000.

A materials handling equipment company reduced the number of days to process an invoice from 22 to 4.5 with the adoption of one simple measuring technique, resulting in a dramatic reduction in outstanding accounts receivable.

A communications firm realized a $3.4 million profit the first year after Chuck applied his measurement expertise. The year before, the company had realized a $1.7 million profit and had never realized more than a $2 million annual profit.

A trucking company reduced maintenance costs by $125,000 a year by charting an item as simple as the number of miles between breakdowns.

Two brothers who were dentists knew they had to do something to increase their production and thought the answer might be to buy into a dental franchise. Their average monthly production totaled about $17,000 a month. After their first month of consulting with The Game of Work, LLC, they were glad they stayed where they were, having had an increase to about $36,000 with the same staff, same doctors, same location.

A young dentist with a staff of two (front desk and chair assistant) had been practicing several years but was unable to break past $10,000 in monthly production. After only four weeks in Chuck Coonradt's program, his production increased to $14,900. Two months later they had the same staff, the same patients, and the same office space, but they were producing over $16,000 a month and were climbing for a new goal of $20,000.

An older dentist was ready to retire in a few years but was not sure how that would ever happen. He said he was already so busy he just couldn't see himself producing more than $30,000 a month without moving to a larger building. The Game of Work began monitoring and measuring his business, and he saw tremendous improvement within the first two months. The third month, his total production was over $50,000.

Success

By following the principles in this book, you can achieve the same kind of dramatic success that these people have achieved. Paul J. Meyer, president of SMI International, says that success is the progressive realization of worthwhile, predetermined personal goals. Napoleon Hill said that success is the pursuit of a worthy ideal. Success is results. That's what we're in business for. In sports, success is measured in touchdowns, in winning the Lombardi Trophy, the Super Bowl, the NBA title, or the Stanley Cup.

If you haven't looked at yourself as a sports entity before, it's time you did. You really are like an athlete in that you have certain talents, abilities, and energy that you market for money and recognition. You are a participant in the game of work, whether you like it or not, and this book is not only about making the cut, but about choosing to become a superstar.

In addition to being responsible for your own growth and development, there may be others whose productivity you are responsible for. If so, the principles discussed in this book are even more important to you. You are a coach as well as a player. Think about how the motivational principles of athletics can apply to your business, and you will have a slight edge as you read this book.

In business, people earning $60,000 a year are *not* three times better than those earning $20,000 a year. They just have a slight edge. They do a few things better. Often the slight edge is nothing more than a better understanding of what their strengths are.

Your Scouting Report

The Dallas Cowboys have been in the playoffs more than any other team in the NFL. One of the keys to their success is the elaborate scouting reports they maintain on not only professional and college athletes but on high-school players as well.

Let's discuss you, your talents, and your abilities. Let's build a scouting report. In the space below, list the talents and abilities you market for money. List the important ones first.

1. _____

2. _____

3. _____

4. _____

5. _____

6. _____

7. _____

8. _____

9. _____

10. _____

Now list the things you have done over the years to improve your talents and abilities. Include schooling, seminars, subscriptions to trade journals, and so on. Beside each list the approximate cost.

1. College   Cost:

2. Post-graduate studies   Cost:

3. Seminars and workshops   Cost:

4. Books   Cost:

5. Trade journals   Cost:

6. Other _____   Cost:

_____   Cost:

_____   Cost:

Your training may have covered:

1. *Know-how or skills*, what you have learned to do.

2. *Energy*, your ability to roll up your sleeves and keep your nose to the grindstone day after day.

3. *Time*, not how much you have, but how well you organize it to make it work for you.

4. *Imagination*, that creative spark, coming up with the ideas nobody else has thought of.

5. *Planning and goal setting*, how well you set goals and develop workable plans to achieve those goals.

6. *Communication skills*, how well you present your ideas and suggestions to others so they are willing to accept and carry out your suggestions.

7. *Decision-making ability*, how well you gather and assimilate facts to make good decisions.

If you could have any one of these talents or abilities in rich abundance, which would it be? Which one, if developed to perfection, would be most useful to you? Of course, you would probably like to see your abilities in all these areas improved, but there is probably one area where you need the most help right now. Which is it?

Write it down here:

Albert Einstein said he developed about ten percent of his potential. What would you guess is your percentage of developed potential right now in the area you selected? What seminars or classes could you take to improve the above talent or ability? How much would that cost in time and money?

You know how much you have invested in this book, and that is only a fraction of what a reputable seminar or college course would cost, yet the principles presented in this book have brought immediate and remarkable improvement to thousands of people. They have worked for others, and they will help you improve in any area you desire.

Goals

Here's something you must consider: All organizations rise or fall on the personal goals of the individuals in that organization. What are your goals? Only three percent of Americans are independently wealthy; they can live off the income from their investment capital. The next ten percent live comfortably, the way most of us would like to live. And 60 percent barely make a living, from one paycheck to the next. The last 27 percent need support from others or the government just to survive. What is the difference between these groups? The top three percent have written, specific goals. They keep score. The next ten percent have goals generally in mind, but they are not *specific* and *written.* The rest have no goals. (See David C. McClelland, *The Achieving Society* [New York: Free Press, 1967]. This has also been verified by subsequent studies.)

Obviously, the achievement of goals involves a lot more than just writing down goals. Otherwise there would be a lot more than three percent in that top group. This book will teach you the precise principles that will help you reach your goals.

The Game of Work is the most effective tool to come into American business in 30 years. The application of measurement and goal setting is not new. But the application of it through the Game of Work is. It has not worked in the past because it has typically been used as punishment or evaluation. Think about how you feel about measurement in numbers. The bad kids in study hall had to report regularly, the good kids got free time. When our business has problems, we send in the auditors and increase the frequency of measurement. But when we ask them to leave the measurement in place, they typically reply, "We'll take it with us, and if you mess up, we'll bring it back." Our measurement and accountability have been viewed too often in a punitive fashion. Thirty-five years ago we rejected Dr. Edward Deming's offer to the American management system and had to send him to Japan for validation before we began to understand how to diagnostically use our measurement system. Also, we have in the past typically reviewed and measured just activity— how fast, how long, how much work did we get involved in. We have not tied measurement to results. And more important, the newness of the Game of Work is tied up in its exciting application of the results to resources ratios, which give everyone that managerial return on investment—that stewardship for results.

The history of performance appraisals has been, in my

opinion, as Shakespeare wrote, "much ado about nothing." We have attempted to adjust the idea of appraisal in a number of ways. In 1892, Frederick Taylor, father of scientific management, said the most important job we have is to determine what a fair day's work is. We have made attempt after attempt to do that. In the 1940s a performance appraisal was the appraisal of the person, and we set goals for unimportant things. In the '50s we talked about management by objective and achievement scales that became a paperwork jungle. Unfortunately, the size of our program was measured by the size of the rings in our binder and not by the results we produced. In the '60s we began using a behavioral approach that said if we do certain things the results surely will follow. But inevitably they didn't. And then we got into performance management, and we still didn't have an understanding of where the goal lines were. In the '70s we began to listen. Finally, Deming's revolutionary Japanese approach—a numbers-based, quality, people-oriented approach—came back to haunt us, and our ignorance of 30 years ago began to cause anguish in the American management system. The measurement of quality began to quantify areas we once thought were immeasurable. We began to get the measurement down to the worker, not just to the quality control inspector. In the '80s the synthesis was beginning to come through. Peter Drucker's mentality first expressed in his book *Managing for Results* is finally bearing fruit. Our experience with all of the other sophistications and complications has brought us full circle to caring about people and letting them care about us and our product response. That's the power in the Game of Work.

In Conclusion

Before you go on to the first chapter, get out of your chair, walk into the bathroom, and look at yourself in the mirror. Say, "I am a player." Say it a couple of times. Set your mind to the idea that you are a true competitor in the game you have freely chosen, and that through your choices in implementing the principles in this book, you will become a winner at the game of work.

1

The Game of Work

*People will pay for the privilege
of working harder than they will work
when they are paid.*

—Chuck Coonradt

In the frozen food business, people are hired to work in refrigerated warehouses in terrible working conditions at near-zero temperatures. But the unions and OSHA have done much to make conditions bearable. Companies are required to provide insulated clothing and boots. In fact, an entire industry provides clothing to companies with refrigerated warehouses. These companies are required to provide hot drinks within so many feet of cold work areas. Workers must have a ten-minute break every hour. It's tough to get people to work in those kinds of conditions. People dislike working in the cold.

Yet whenever a winter snowstorm passes over my home in the mountains, followed by clearing skies and plunging temperatures, there is a sudden jump in employee absenteeism, particularly among young workers. Instead of staying home to avoid the freezing temperatures, they migrate up the local canyons to test the new and famous powder snow at Alta, Snowbird, or Park City.

Equipped with hundreds of dollars' worth of equipment, they gladly take a reduction in pay for the day off and buy a $30 pass to spend the day outside in subfreezing temperatures. There are no hot-drink vending machines on the slopes, nor have I ever heard of a skier demanding a ten-minute break every hour. People really will pay for the privilege of working harder than they will work when they are paid.

Consider deer hunting. Every year during the third week in October, hundreds of thousands of men drag themselves to work Monday through Thursday. They are slow, lethargic, saving energy for the weekend. Then on Thursday afternoon, it's as if every one of them takes some kind of magic energy pill. Their eyes open wide. They stay up all night cleaning rifles, sharpening knives, waterproofing boots, and loading the camper with hundreds of dollars' worth of food. Friday morning they spend five or six hours driving along the roughest roads in the world, often in snowstorms. The next morning, the same men who on workdays have trouble fixing a bowl of cold cereal are up at 4 a.m. fixing a huge breakfast of bacon, eggs, fried potatoes, juice, and hot drinks.

After breakfast they wander out into a freezing blizzard, hoping for a chance to drag a dead deer through places they wouldn't carry their dying friend—all the time pretending the meat they might get is an economical investment to cut future grocery bills. Those hunters pay for the privilege of working harder than they will work when they are paid.

But why? Why do people put up to ten times as much energy and effort into their avocations as into their vocations? Why will people pay for the privilege of working harder than they will work when they are paid? There are several reasons.

First, *in recreation goals are clearly defined:* Shooting a deer; winning a game; beating your previous time. The desired result is clear and easily measured.

I've always wanted to play the Pebble Beach Golf Course in Carmel, California. That's where they hold the annual Bing Crosby Pro-Am tournament.

Let's assume I finally make it to the course.

"I'm here to play," I say. "Where is a map of the course?"

"We don't have a map of the course anymore," says the attendant at the door.

"How do I know where to play? Where's the first tee?" I ask.

"Well, we changed," she says. "With property values so high we have converted half the course into condos. As a result, we've changed the rules some. There's no longer a first tee."

"Well, do you have a second tee?"

"We don't have a second tee, either. In fact, we don't have any tees anymore."

"Uh, well, what about the greens?"

"Don't have those either."

"Are the boundaries gone too?"

"Yes, except that it's off limits to hit a ball into somebody's yard."

"How do I play?"

"Well," she says, "we've analyzed why people play golf, and the big reason is exercise. Here's a pedometer. Go out and walk 6,700 yards wherever you wish. You won't need a caddy because you only need to take along one club. Stop and swing it whenever you wish, a minimum of 70 times or until you feel like you've had the normal amount of exercise for an 18-hole game of golf."

"You're kidding!" I say.

"But the activity is still the same," she continues. "You still get the exercise, you still swing the club (you can even throw one if you want to), and you don't ever have to go look for a lost ball."

Can you imagine someone actually saying that? Or can you imagine going out on the soccer field and hearing someone say, "Listen, mostly this game is running and exercise. We don't want to do all the accounting, so we just took the goals out. You can run around kicking the ball for 45 minutes, then we'll take a break. Then you can run around another 45 minutes. After that you can go home and tell everyone how well you exercised."

If you took the measurements out of the New York Marathon, there is no way in the world you'd ever get 20,000 people to stand and wait two hours on the Brooklyn Bridge in the predawn hours for a chance to run 26 miles.

Second, *in recreation the scorekeeping is better* because it's

(1) more objective, (2) self- administered, (3) peer audited, (4) dynamic, and (5) it allows the player to compare current personal performance with past personal performance as well as an accepted standard.

In recreation, everybody knows how to keep score. In business, however, sometimes the strokes don't count. Frequently workers don't understand the scorekeeping system. Sometimes nobody cares. Frequently there is too little objectivity in business scorekeeping.

I play golf with a handicap of 18. If I break 85 on 18 holes I'm in heaven. But sometimes I play with friends who claim handicaps of eight or ten. If they hit 85, they are losing and are disappointed.

In golf you get realistic feedback that you can relate to your own past performance. If you were getting feedback on your golf game comparing you to Jack Nicklaus, you would soon become discouraged and quit because you could never win. But accurate feedback related to your own past performance usually gives you enough positive reinforcement to make you want to keep playing, to keep improving, to beat your own past performance standards. You win frequently enough to want to keep playing.

Have you ever met a runner who couldn't tell you how fast he runs his miles? Anybody can be a jogger—just shuffle along and you've got it. But a runner must run miles in less than eight minutes. Every serious runner keeps score. If you consistently run eight-minute miles, then you really feel good about yourself if you finish a workout averaging 7:40-minute miles. And if you break seven, that's all you can talk about all day. You don't feel bad because you didn't break the four-minute mile, or because you are not running marathons in two hours. You feel great because you are measuring yourself against your own past performance and winning. If you ran your last marathon in 4:10, then you feel great when you break four hours. You don't feel let down if you didn't make 2:40. You feel like a winner because you are not comparing your performance to some unrealistic standard.

Consider a volunteer civic tennis tournament sponsored by a local television station every summer that draws, 2,700 participants with only four people keeping score. In a professional golf tournament with 140 participants, there are three people keeping score, and they sit in a tent and never see a stroke. Why? Because the scorecards are self-administered and peer audited.

In recreation, the scorekeeping enables you to receive immediate and realistic feedback. You know at all times how you are doing.

Imagine that you are on the golf course playing for $20 a hole. You have two holes left to play and you're behind, so you talk your opponent into pressing the bet—double the bet on the last two holes in an effort to catch up.

You step up to the tee and blast the ball over the fence. You don't have to wait until the next six-month interview with the golf pro to know you blew it. You have been keeping your own score on every hole and know exactly where you stand.

You feel bad, not because you didn't play as well as Jack Nicklaus, but because you didn't play up to your personal expectations corresponding to your handicap.

Scorekeeping is an effective form of motivation if it is objective, self-administered, and peer audited.

Third, *in recreation feedback is more frequent.* Everybody needs to know every day whether he is winning or losing. What do you think would happen if the commissioner of pro football walked onto the field at the beginning of the annual Super Bowl game to determine the best football team in the world, and said to the players, "We're going to be more businesslike in our approach to football today. We're not going to keep score. The commissioners are just going to watch the game, then meet and decide which team played the best. We'll let you know what we decide within three months." The commissioner would have to run for his life!

Fortunately, in most recreational activities you don't have to depend on a boss or supervisor to tell you how you are doing. You know what the score is as the game progresses, and nobody can change that just because they don't like you. The feedback is accurate and frequent—you know where you stand every time you throw the ball. And everybody knows how to keep score.

Feedback is the breakfast of champions. People who want to get ahead, who want to win, who want to improve and get the job done—these people want feedback. If you don't think feedback is important, go count the mirrors in your house.

If you want to improve the quality of performance in any area, you simply improve or increase the frequency of feedback. If you have a problem and you are getting a quarterly report, change it to a monthly report. If that doesn't do the job, turn it into a weekly or daily report. By increasing the frequency of your feedback, you have more opportunities to catch and eliminate problems of a solvable size.

Fourth, *in recreation participants feel they have a higher degree of choice.* Think about the words that imply a lack of choice—words frequently used in business. Words like "have to," "should," "must." How many times have you heard someone say, "I have to go play tennis?"

I'm a tennis player, and I don't think golfers get much exercise. They hit the ball, get in the cart, get out of the cart, hit the ball again, and get back in the cart. Racquetballers don't think tennis players get much exercise. We stand around, only half of the serves count, and we chase the ball half of the time. Handballers say real players don't need racquets to beat up on a little bitty ball. Part of the reason for liking a recreational activity is the free choice you have in electing to do it.

Managers must ask themselves if they are using the principle of choice when giving out assignments to employees. Are people being allowed to perform in areas where they have natural interests and abilities, or is their business like the Army where bakers are ordered to drive trucks? When people feel that they have no choice in what they are doing, they lose their enthusiasm, and performance suffers.

Fifth, *in recreation they don't change the rules in the middle of the game.* Imagine that you are playing pool in a strange town and winning. You just put in the eighth ball when somebody announces that it didn't count because you didn't say "Molly

Mumford" before it went in the hole. Obviously you are upset because someone changed the rules on you. That doesn't happen in sports. If the basketball goes through the hoop, you get two points. The pros and some college leagues have three-point baskets, but the rules for getting three-point baskets are set up during the off season, never in the middle of a game. In business, however, rules are frequently changed in the middle of the game.

One time I sat down with a regional sales manager for a light bulb manufacturer. We were talking about scorekeeping and maintaining a high motivational level among the salespeople.

"We have a good scorekeeping system," he said. "Our people get regular reports listing their point accumulations, yet the system doesn't seem to motivate our people."

"That sounds strange," I said, because it appeared to be a good scorekeeping system.

Then he said, "I guess the thing they are upset about is the Annual National Quota Adjustment."

"What?" I said.

"Annual National Quota Adjustment," he repeated matter-of-factly, as if I ought to be familiar with the term.

"Tell me about it," I said.

"If the whole company," he explained, "does 125 percent of quota, then we depreciate the value of everybody's points back down to the 100 percent level."

"It's obvious to me," I said, "that your people can't count on a stroke being a stroke. You are changing the rules in the middle of the game."

Consider a grocery store where the meat manager has just been chewed out by the store manager for not making enough money on the meat.

"We're going to fix this," says the store manager to the meat manager. "We're going to pinch every nickel and dime in this department, and we are going to start making some money!" The meat manager nods in agreement.

Mrs. Jones comes in the store an hour later with a bad ham. She goes back to the meat manager, who has just had the rules laid down about watching the pennies. The manager gives her a hard time about exchanging the ham. She gives up and goes to the store manager, who says, "No problem, Mrs. Jones. I'll take you back and explain to that stupid meat manager of mine how we are going to have customer satisfaction around here." The store manager has changed the rules in the middle of the game.

Now, if they changed the rules in a football game, the referee saying after a touchdown that the ball carrier got into the end zone too easily, so the touchdown would be worth only four points, what do you think would happen?

Changing the rules in the middle of the game adds to the uncertainty of the game. Good managers seek to minimize uncertainty. Workers, like athletes, perform better when they know where they stand, when they know the score. A feeling of certainty creates a sense of security about working conditions. Managers cannot eliminate all uncertainty, but by avoiding changing the rules in the middle of the game, they can go a long way toward minimizing uncertainty.

In the workplace, when expectations are clearly defined and uncertainty is minimized, it is easier for people to have the satisfaction of meeting expectations.

What do you think happens when these five principles are applied in the working world—when we apply the motivation of recreation to work? Can you imagine the enthusiasm level in your organization being as great for the accomplishment of your goals as you get in the bowling league or the company bridge tournament?

There's a productivity crisis in America. We hear about it every day. Yet while our workers become less productive, recreational interests and abilities are growing by leaps and bounds.

If the office air conditioning goes off on a hot day, and if it's 100 degrees outside, soon the temperature of the office gets up to about 80 degrees. People start tugging at their collars, saying "Boy, it's tough working in here. We'd better go home early."

We all agree that it's tough to work when the temperature gets up to 80 degrees. But the minute we step outside where it's 100 degrees, somebody says, "What do you think, golf or tennis?"

The principles that lead to motivation in recreation can be applied to business with remarkable results. In this book I will uncover and define those principles, then teach you how to apply them.

Professional athletes are paid to play. But the enthusiasm and the power of their involvement come from the elements of the game, not the amount of the paycheck. Each of us is paid to play as well. But we can increase our enthusiasm, we can increase our enjoyment, we can increase our self-fulfillment by implementing the principles of the Game of Work. In this book you will find the way to win at your personal Game of Work. I guarantee it.

2

Goals

In the absence of clearly defined goals,
we are forced to concentrate on activity
and ultimately become enslaved by it.

—Chuck Coonradt

Let's take a look at what goal-setting does in athletics. If you took the goals out of football, what would you have? You would give the Lombardi Trophy to the team each year that racked up the most yardage—and if you took the yard markers off the field, you would have to give it to the team that could stay on the field the longest. Then football would be like many businesses that use longevity as the main criteria for promotion.

If you took the goals out of basketball, you would have ten guys running up and down the floor just dribbling the ball—as we do in business sometimes, but without the ball.

If you took the goals out of hockey, you would have 12 players on the ice fighting, and some people think that would improve the sport. Everything we do in our recreational pursuits is absolutely and totally goal directed. In hunting we have the Boone and Crockett Club to record the largest, widest, and best antler spread and the highest quality trophy taken. Thousands of work hours a week are spent updating the NFL record book.

If you took the goals out of any sport, you would remove the most significant aspect of recreational pursuits—goal setting and goal-striving. There is something inherent in us to want to do things better, faster, higher, shorter, longer—and to win.

When John Nabors set up a three-year training program after seeing Mark Spitz win his gold medals in the previous Olympics, John didn't just want to become a good swimmer. He didn't just climb in the pool and swim his heart out twice a day for 165 weeks for the fun of it. He didn't do it because it was great exercise. He did it because he had a specific goal to become the best in the world at his event.

Goals are the motivating force in athletics. And in athletics, goals are more clearly defined than in business. Goals are the main reason people will pay for the privilege of working harder than they will work when they are paid.

When we walk onto the tennis court, we know the goal is to win. When we go onto a football or soccer field, we know where we have to put ourselves and what our performance has to be to score. We must have that same challenge, that same opportunity, that same motivation when we walk into the office in the morning—instead of waiting for the phone to ring or the mail to hit the desk to get things happening.

Goals in recreation are clearly defined, and as a result motivation in recreation is at a higher level than in business. Can we bring the motivation of recreation into the workplace? Absolutely!

When the following criteria for goal-setting are applied in the workplace, they can produce motivation similar to that found in recreation.

1. *Goals must be written.* Mike Holmgren, after his Green Bay Packers won Super Bowl XXXI said it was because they attended every practice, chalk talk, and prepared for every game with the well organized specific written goals.

People will often avoid writing goals, saying, "I don't need to write anything. I can keep my important goals in my head. I can concentrate on the things that are really meaningful in my life." But if the phone rings in the middle of that conversation and their spouse is on the other end asking them to pick up five items from the grocery store, they say, "Hold it. Let me write this down so I won't forget."

Goals that are not written are merely wishes. There is something in the act of writing a goal down that makes it real, gives it permanence, removes it from the realm of fleeting whims. Goals that are not written down are easily forgotten or changed; written goals that are reviewed regularly become reality. Unwritten goals cannot be read and reviewed. When goals are not written, the power of conditioning through spaced repetition is lost.

I am continuously amazed how people, after paying huge tuitions to attend seminars on goal setting, resist writing their goals. They must think the Super Bowl Champions make up their plays during their games. Ridiculous. The main difference between professional and sandlot football is the amount of written documentation of their plans.

A team's goal is not just to win the championship or to be the best. Good goals are detailed and specific—yards per carry, number of offensive and defensive plays, plays per series. Goals must be broken down into a specific plan, in writing.

It is impossible to manage anything in violation of the principle of written goals. None of us would build a $200,000 house without a set of plans from the architect. But most average workers earning $20,000 a year for ten years ($200,000) will spend it without specific goals or plans and then wonder at the end of the ten years why they have gained nothing more than the appreciation on their house. Goals must be written.

2. *Goals must be your own.* Super Bowl rings are won by individual players. The greatest successes in sports are the result of individual commitments to personal success.

Franz Klammer, the Austrian Gold Medal Champion who roared to victory in the downhill of the winter Olympics, fell behind the leading pace by one-fifth of a second—a huge margin in downhill skiing. The course was covered with icy ruts from previous skiers, and the fog had moved in, making it impossible for a skier to see more than two flags at one time. But Klammer's mighty exertion in the last thousand meters enabled him to tie and then beat the best time by one-third of a second. Later, Klammer said, "When I left the gate, I decided that I would win or die." He won.

I remember the seventh game of the 1977 World Series. The Yankees were playing the Dodgers in Yankee Stadium. Up until that game, Reggie Jackson was not having a great series. He was catching a lot of flak in the New York press. In game seven he hit three home runs, leading the Yankees to victory. Why did Reggie do so well? For his team? Possibly. For George Steinbrenner? Certainly not. He did it for Reggie Jackson.

Whose company do I work for? Mine. Whose boss do I work for? Mine. Whose income am I most concerned about? Mine. I, me, my, mine. Whose goals are the most important to me? Mine.

You no doubt have observed people who go through life giving just the minimum daily requirement at work, and yet when the whistle sounds, they are off to coach a Little League team, play in a bowling league, build a mountain cabin—do something that is uniquely theirs. You've noticed the transformation, the new energy, the intelligence, the creativity, the endurance, and the capacity for work. It's awesome.

Goal-setting and goal-striving become truly effective only when team or corporate goals become the same as personal goals—when it becomes my team or my company. If you look at the employees of the finest organizations, the ones that we admire, they talk about "my company." These employees have entrepreneurial instincts to help ensure the success of their companies because their personal goals are intertwined with the company goals.

3. *Goals must be positive.* Vince Lombardi said that the objective of the game is to win— fairly, squarely, and by the rules, but to win. The goal in sports is not to avoid a loss or defeat. How many times have you seen professional golfers changing their game plan to protect their lead instead of going for everything they can get, only to see the lead slip away? They get beaten because they lose the momentum of their earlier positive attack.

The batting average is an excellent example of a positive goal. Consider Tony Gwynn and Wade Boggs, who have had the highest season averages and won more batting titles than any other players in the recent history of the game. Neither has been able to bat above the mystical .400 mark, the goal achieved by Ted Williams. We consider the .400 average a positive goal. We don't look at that magical mark as being wrong 60 percent of the time. In baseball we keep track of hits and home runs, not strikeouts.

The two most common goals in America are to quit smoking and to lose weight—both negative. I used to smoke—and talk about a habit reinforced by spaced repetition. A pack a day, 365 days a year—7,300 times a year, reaching for the smokes. The problem is getting your arm to quit moving from pocket to mouth.

Rather than have the negative goal to quit smoking, someone who wants to stop must have a goal to become a nonsmoker. Nonsmokers have tremendous benefits. They get lower rates on life and car insurance. Their clothes last longer. They don't ruin furniture or carpets. Their smell is not offensive to others. They are nonsmokers, a positive thing to be.

The problem is that most people who quit smoking still see themselves as smokers on vacation or on the wagon, and it is just a matter of time until they start up again.

I once knew a young man who told me he smoked between a pack and a half and two packs of cigarettes a day. When I said "Oh, 35 cigarettes a day," he looked at me and said, "Oh, no. It couldn't possibly be that many." But if a pack and a half is 30, and two packs is 40, then somewhere between the two is 35.

As he began to clearly identify the magnitude of his habit, he then started graphing and tracking his progress to smoke a predetermined number of cigarettes a day.

The first day, I suggested that he smoke 35, his average in the past and something that wouldn't present any challenge. He called me at ten o'clock that night asking, "Do I have to smoke all 35? I'm up to 32, and, frankly, I've had enough." To make him successful in his attempt to reach a predetermined goal, I insisted he smoke all 35, which he did.

The next day he set a goal of 34 cigarettes. Now you might say, "Ah, clever, you're asking him to cut back a cigarette a day." No, I'm asking him to smoke a predetermined number of cigarettes each day so he can get it into his mind that he can determine in his own mind how many he will smoke every day. With that positive attitude and conditioning, his goal went to 32 a day, 31, and 30.

After two weeks he said he wanted to quit, but I said no because I knew he needed more reinforcement before he stopped something he had been doing almost 13,000 times a year for many years. Every morning as he decided how many cigarettes and at which times he would smoke, he always kept the after-dinner smoke at the end of his list. He learned to smoke as many cigarettes as he decided each morning. When his goal finally was to smoke zero cigarettes a day, he could truly in his own mind say, "I am a nonsmoker."

The same principle applies to losing weight. Imagine losing twenty pounds. What are you going to do? Cut off an arm? Sometimes many of us feel that would be less painful than the way we go about it. Instead of a negative goal in pounds that need to be lost, the goal must be to achieve an optimal weight and to maintain that weight once it is achieved.

The problem people have with losing weight is that after they take it off they go out and celebrate by stuffing it back on again with hot-fudge sundaes and lemon meringue pies—at least those are my favorites. You must be able to visualize the goal, and the only way the goal can be visual is if it is positive.

In basketball and football they count the points you score, not the ones you miss. But in life many times we will do 80 percent of the task and then when asked to report on it say, "Nope, I failed."

We must be willing, as the old song says, to accentuate the positive. The mind rejects negative goals; they are hard to visualize.

4. *Goals must be measurable and specific.* In sports we demand numbers—two, three, and even four places to the right of the decimal point. Strokes in golf are no longer a small enough measurement. It's hundredths of strokes that count. The times of swimmers, speed skaters, and downhill skiers are all measured in thousandths of seconds, and in order to separate one athlete from

the others these kinds of exact measurements are essential.

How much, how many, and by when? If you can't measure it, how will you know when you achieved it? Even intangible goals need tangible indicators. If you have a goal to be more patient, count how many times you raise your voice in a month. If the numbers drop, your patience is increasing. Don't say, "I am going to do better next year," but "I am going to make X number of calls next year."

Paul J. Meyer insists, "Definite goals produce definite results. On the other hand, indefinite goals do not produce indefinite results. They produce no results at all."

If you put 100 people in a room and ask them how many would like to be financially independent, all the hands will go up. If you then ask how many have a personal financial statement detailing assets, liabilities, and net worth that is current in the last 90 days—and I don't mean the paper they had to fill out to get a loan at the bank—90 of those 100 people will not raise their hands.

If you ask those remaining ten people how many have that financial statement laid out in a pro-forma goals format for one-, three-, five-, ten-, and 20-year periods, nine of the people will sit down. The one still standing will be a millionaire. It does not make any difference what the person's background is, how much money the person has, or what the person's current income is. That person has a plan, and because of that, you cannot turn the person aside. Goals must answer the questions how much, how many, and by when.

If your company philosophy claims that the customer is king, then you may want to measure the percentage of orders coming from repeat customers, the size of orders per customer, or the number of complaints per thousand transactions and how you dealt with them. Unless the overall goals of the company reflect how much, how many, by when, and by whom, you don't really have legitimate goals.

5. *Goals are best stated in inflation-proof terms.* We've discussed the elusive goal of a .400 batting average—an inflation-proof goal that has not changed in 40 years since Ted Williams

achieved it. Salaries and commissions may go up or down. Ticket prices may go up, but some things are always the same—minutes, hours, pounds, hits, baskets, touchdowns. Goals are best stated in units of measurement that don't change.

There is a paper company in the Northwest that decided to produce fine paper. They had already been in the pulp business for many years, and they were accustomed to measuring production in tons, not dollars.

Back in the late '60s, the fine paper division was established. They took a controller out of headquarters and sent her over to run the new division. She was tonnage oriented, not dollar oriented, when it came to measuring production.

She was told that in the fine paper industry, everything was measured in dollar value. She said, "No, we're going to count pounds and tons, even in the sales department."

About this time, a sudden paper shortage appeared worldwide, and paper prices increased dramatically. While everyone else was measuring dollar sales volumes and patting themselves on the backs with 13 and 14 percent sales increases each year when prices were going up 20 and 30 percent a year, the workers at this new fine paper division were hustling to beat pound quotas. While inflation lulled the bulk of the fine paper companies into a false sense of security, this company was capturing a huge share of the market. They'd set their goals in noninflationary numbers.

The majority of retail stores in the United States today have not managed to have their sales per customer keep up with the increases in inflation. The actual tonnage or amount of product sold in these stores has actually decreased while dollar sales have increased. Most of them have actually been behind on the scoreboard and didn't even know it, thanks to inflation and shortsighted management. Inflation is a fact. It can be good or bad, but it is a real force in business. Only when we can take it out of our goals program, as that paper company did, can we be the beneficiaries rather than the victims of inflation.

6. *Goals must be stated in the most visible terms available.* When goals are measured in real things, everybody knows the

score. When the points go up on an NFL scoreboard, everybody knows what is happening, who is ahead, and who is catching up or widening their lead.

Goals must be measured in something you can see. Percentages are too vague. The sales representative may say to the sales manager after a long period of thought and soul searching, "My goal is to increase my volume by 25 percent."

"Great," responds the sales manager. "According to my records, last January you achieved 10,000 unit sales. According to your goal you'll get 12,500 this January. Fantastic!"

"Wait a minute," says the sales rep. "There's no way I'll get 12,500 in January, but the 25 percent increase will be a cinch."

Nonsense. The person may have a nebulous feeling that somehow the sales can be made up in December, but that won't happen if he or she is afraid in January to face the goal in real numbers. Even dollars are better than percentages. Goals must be stated in pounds, units, calls, boxes—things you can see and touch.

Organizations can measure labor in at least four different ways:

1. Labor costs in relation to dollar sales. (Most accountants prefer this measurement.)
2. Dollar sales per person-hour.
3. Invoices or customers served per person-hour.
4. Pounds or tons produced per person-hour.

The cost of labor and dollar sales are both inflationary indicators and therefore can get very complicated and hard to figure. If wage costs and sales prices do not change in a parallel fashion, you end up comparing apples to oranges. In comparing labor costs to dollar sales you are using two variables, both of which are subject to inflationary changes. You are better off comparing dollar sales to person-hours so only the first variable is vulnerable to change due to inflation. Hours are easy to measure because they are non-inflationary: there will never be more than 60 minutes in an hour. Other noninflationary variable units include invoices, customers, pounds, and tons.

I once asked a group of managers how many hours a week a store would have to cut out to have a one percent labor savings if

I once asked a group of managers how many hours a week a store would have to cut out to have a 1-percent labor savings if it had labor costs of $10,000 a week and paid its employees $5 an hour.

The responses were incredible. One manager asked me for a calculator. Another said I hadn't given enough information to solve the problem. Another asked what kind of business it was. None could quickly come up with what seemed to be a very simple answer. One percent of $10,000 is $100. At $5 an hour, to save $100 in a week the company would have to drop twenty hours from the schedule.

But managers shouldn't have to translate, even simple problems like this one. In the heat of competition, communications have to be direct and simple, like the bidding at a bridge tournament.

In that same industry one of our clients came up with a "customers served per person-hour" measurement. It was easy to measure the number of customers per hour and at the same time know how many employees were on duty. At the end of each day the manager figured the customers served per person-hour, and future work schedules were planned accordingly.

The point is that labor-control goals are best accomplished by using specific, easily measured quantities. Managers don't have to translate. Audibles cannot be called at the line of scrimmage, as is sometimes necessary, unless everyone has been told their meaning before the game begins.

7. *Goals must contain a deadline.* Remember the 1980 Holiday Bowl between Southern Methodist University and Brigham young University in San Diego? With three minutes and fifty-seven seconds remaining in the game, SMU was ahead 45-25. The fans were starting to leave, figuring there was no way SMU could lose.

On the following series BYU drove the length of the field and scored on a pass from Jim McMahon (seventy NCAA records) to Matt Bragga. BYU failed on a two-point conversion effort, then succeeded in getting the ball back on an inside kick. Several plays later McMahon threw a forty-yard pass. On the next play BYU scored again and succeeded in the two-point conversion. The score was now 45-39 with less than two minutes to play. This time the onside kick failed and SMU got the ball, forcing BYU to use its last time-out as SMU let the clock run to the maximum on four plays before punting. BYU blocked the punt and got the ball back midfield with eighteen seconds remaining in the game. On the first play McMahon threw the ball away. Eleven seconds remained. On the second play he threw it out of bounds. Three seconds remained.

After taking the next snap, McMahon dropped back farther than usual, allowing receivers time to get downfield. Then he threw a perfect, sixty-yard-strike, right in front of the goalposts. All-American tight end Clay Brown was the intended receiver. Surrounded by SMU defenders, he leaped into the air, no time remaining on the clock, and brought down the pass. BYU won the game.

If you don't have a deadline, you don't have a goal. Goals must say how much, how many, and *by when.*

The most exciting play in all of sports occurs in that last two minutes before the half, or the last two minutes before the end of any given period, whether it is a hockey, basketball, or football game.

Deadlines allow the student who has slept in all term, not able to get out of bed before 10 a.m., to stay up all night studying for a midterm exam. Deadlines account for forty percent of the money raised in any telethon to be raised during the last twenty percent of the time. Deadlines are covered in one of Murphy's Laws that says, "The first ten percent of a project requires ninety percent of the time allowed for the entire project to be completed. The second 90 percent requires 90 percent of the time allowed for it, and that's why it takes twice as long as it should."

Deadlines are the foundation of commitment. Deadlines are the adrenalin boosters. Deadlines are the instigators of achievement and inventiveness. A goal without a deadline is merely a philosophical statement.

8. *Goals must allow for personality changes.* In 1977 when fullback Todd Christensen was drafted by the Dallas Cowboys, he was told they were going to switch him to tight end. No, he

him up, tried him at fullback, then cut him. Finally Todd was picked up by the Raiders, whose offensive philosophy is most similar to Brigham Young University, where Christensen played his college ball. Seven years later Todd Christensen was the leading receiver in the NFL and named to the pro all-star team as a tight end.

You must change too, like starting to get up at 6 a.m., working a full day, cutting out the long lunches.

If you double your income next year, how will you spend it? Where will you put it? Unless you've got someplace for it to go, there's no reason to do it or make it. The reason most of us don't make more money than we do right now is because we don't know what we'd do if we had it. It sounds odd, but it's true.

J. Paul Getty wrote a book called *Being Rich.* Not *Getting Rich*, but *Being Rich.* He talked about responsibilities of wealth and the personality traits necessary to develop and manage wealth. Paul Meyer said, "You must first set those goals to *become* before you attempt to set goals to *have.*"

The goals to become are the intangible characteristics that make winners what they are. You cannot, for example, become a great skier if you have a strong fear of injury.

If you take average people in an average job earning an average income, you can guess that they will probably never get ahead as long as things stay the same. But if they find themselves in a traumatic situation, maybe a costly divorce, a major operation without insurance to cover the costs, any financially taxing situation, then they will rise to the increased need and generate an increased income. Or they might fall back into the role of a loser and look to someone else, or the government, to meet their obligations. But we can and do change with goals or traumatic experiences. Winners are champions of change and choice.

9. *Goals must contain an interrelated statement of benefits.* Goals and benefits go together. The acronym WIIFM stands for, "What's in it for me?" Make sure you've got some WIIFM in your goals program.

There is no question that Olympic athletes are motivated by the thrill of the chase, honor of country, and the desire to stand on that medal podium at the highest level. But all of us know that the gold translates into "green" in the form of contracts for endorsements, appearances and products. One of the great benefits of our capitalistic system is the opportunity to keep the WIIFM in all we do.

When I turn in my sales goal, I translate the bottom line into dollars, break it down into a budget (what I will need to live on), and then decide what I want to do with the rest of it.

When preparing your goals, take out a chunk of money just for you after all the living expenses are covered. If it isn't big enough, and you're a salesperson, go back to the sales manager and ask for permission to raise your goal. Take a paramedic with you.

WIIFM explains the *why* to people. Anybody, when asked to do something unusual or out of the ordinary, wants to know *why*. They are not as interested in the *how*. Too often we think communication is poor when we are trying to shove the *how* down someone's throat when they are still waiting to hear the *why*. But if we can clearly define the *why*, then we will have the kind of performance we want and the *how* will pretty much take care of itself.

Too often we think our communications are not being received or that people are resistant to our requests. This happens most when we are trying to shove something down someone's throat when they still don't understand *why* it's important. The great paradox is that when something didn't get done, we go back and ask, "*Why* didn't you do it?"

The *why* in sports is apparent. You wouldn't think of going on a basketball court except to win. You wouldn't think of being in a race unless it was to win or to get a better time. You would not think of going hunting unless you hoped to come home with something other than sore feet. The *why* is such an integral part of recreation that we sometimes overlook its significance. The *why* also needs to be in personal, business, and volunteer activities. Any goal without a benefit statement has no motivational value. Goals must be realistic and obtainable, and they must also carry a promise of reward if achieved.

A good idea in setting goals is to establish an arbitrary

reward for yourself when the goal is accomplished. All of us go through life spending money—house payment, groceries, utilities, car payments, clothing. How exciting. When was the last time you told your spouse you couldn't wait to finish dinner so you could sit down at the desk and pay the gas bill?

There's nothing inherently exciting about going out to buy a new business wardrobe. But it can be exciting if it's a reward for reaching a goal. I'd rather buy a suit as a reward for accomplishing something important to me than because the store puts them on sale. I might pay a little more, but every time I put on that suit the success I enjoyed in reaching the goal will be reinforced. When you have a tangible reward, reaching a goal becomes a *want to* instead of a *have to* experience, and that makes a big difference.

If you enjoy great music, go out and buy yourself a favorite CD or tape after reaching a goal. Write on the cover why you bought it. When you get down in the dumps and can't get yourself going, get out your recordings and listen to them. While you're listening, read what you have written on the covers and remember how you achieved those records. You won't be down in the dumps after half an hour or half a day of that kind of conditioning. The good get better when they celebrate their victories. And if you have tangible memories of your victories you won't forget them.

10. *Goals must be realistic and obtainable.* In football, goals are usually made by a yard here, a yard there. Woody Hayes, one of the great legends in college football, is famous for the phrase "three yards and a cloud of dust." With that concept Woody dominated Big 10 football for decades. The three-yards-and-a-cloud-of-dust attitude will get you further than any instant accomplishment or get-rich-quick scheme.

If you've never earned very much over $50,000 a year and you've established that as your average for a long time, don't suddenly decide that overnight your earning level will jump to $100,000. Most of us are not capable of making the personality and the work habit changes necessary to have such a sudden change in earning ability. But if you set realistic goals and work on them and work on them and work on them, you can get big results. It's like those IRA advertisements. They say if you start making small deposits at age 25 and stick with it, you will be a millionaire by the time you retire. Paul Meyer calls that progressive realization. I call it the secret of success. There is a million dollars in your head, if you can just figure out how to get it out. Keep after it.

Generally, reading a self-help book or taking a motivation course produces little real change. Change is hard to achieve, frequently like that final yard into the end zone in a championship game. But the more realistic and attainable your goals are, the greater your chance of seeing some change, at least a little.

Every company must have overall organizational goals, followed by divisional and departmental ones, and then the individual goals of each member of the organization. All those goals must work together.

Sometimes when companies get down to the departmental goals, they think that is where goal-setting stops. Supervisors are told not to interfere with the private goals of individuals, not to get too close. That's bunk. *Individual goals are the foundation of corporate human-resource development and planning.*

Individuals are motivated by needs and wants. An organization that not only understands the needs and wants of its workers but to a certain degree even influences those wants will be better able to get maximum productivity out of those workers.

Many of us are trained from early childhood not to want. Maybe a well-meaning Sunday school teacher implied that we cannot be rich and righteous at the same time. But we cannot increase our motivation until we increase our desires. Having goals means having desires.

The clear definition of individual goals is the foundation of teamwork. One time an NBA team lost its all-pro point guard at the beginning of the semifinal playoff series. The other starters changed their play to compensate for the loss of the guard, and the team lost the first three games. It wasn't until the coach put in the backup point guard and told the team to play as if the star was in, that the team finally came together and pushed the series to seven games. *Teamwork is based on great individual execution of assigned responsibilities, not compromise and cooperation.* The minute an offensive tackle looks back to try to cover up for a quarterback who can't take the snap, he is compromising his effectiveness as a tackle and usually winds up on his back watching the quarterback get sacked. Only when everyone excels at an assigned task do we have true teamwork.

The success achieved by the U.S. women's volleyball team is directly related to the ability of the spotter to place the ball at a predetermined height over the net from which those leaping front line players can direct it or spike it into the opponents' court. If the spiker was required to compromise her leaping ability to cooperate with the setter's inability to perform, we would have another also-ran performance. In business, effective organizations are those that have the ability to produce and deliver the product at the exact moment the salespeople promised it would arrive. I was shocked when working with a custom manufacturing company to hear that on-time delivery was not *that* important because the salespeople had developed the ability to talk customers into an extended delivery date. They had actually built a corporate culture of compromise. That is not winning behavior.

On your team, in your business, you cannot achieve great teamwork unless the goals are clearly defined down to the individual level. That is your challenge if you want the motivation of recreation in your business or organization.

3

Scorekeeping

If you can't measure it, you can't manage it.

—George Odiorne

Have you ever noticed the difference between figure skating and ice hockey crowds? The figure skating crowd offers polite applause when they see a good skating exhibition. The ice hockey fans scream and yell when they see something they like, or don't like, on the ice. What's the difference? Both sports take place on the ice and both involve skilled skaters who have spent many years in preparing to perform.

One reason figure skating crowds are so timid is that they don't know for sure what is happening on the ice. They know that someone is skating, but they don't know the score. After the skating is over, the judges flip up their cards—5.7, 5.6, 5.2, 6.0. It is such a bad system that they throw out the high and low scores. And the skater doesn't know if he's ahead or behind until it's too late to do anything about it. It's a terrible scorekeeping system, but until something better comes along, we'll have to live with it.

Ice hockey is different. Every fan and every player knows the score at all times. The team that is ahead knows it and takes appropriate action to protect that lead. The team that's behind knows the score too and can take catch-up action. The fans know the score and can cheer their team to victory.

Scorekeeping is the heart of athletics, and it must be the heart of every successful business. What is the first thing news reports mention about any sporting event? The score: who won, the points earned by each team. Then come the stats, the specific measurements of individual and team accomplishments. In sports, we start with the scoreboard page and add the editorial comment. Too often in business we get this reversed.

In sports, especially professional sports, measurements are continually added to increase interest in the game. Baseball has added what they call the slugging percentage, in addition to the batting average and runs batted in. Golf has added driving accuracy, putting percentages, number of greens hit, and putts per round. Some basketball coaches are monitoring points per possession in an effort to measure the effectiveness of both offensive and defensive strategies.

Every sport has its scorecards, scoreboards, and stat sheets—and so must every business. Business managers must be on constant lookout for new measurements to improve productivity.

The primary responsibility of managers is to set the rules and create the scorecards. Archaic scorekeeping systems, or no systems at all, force employees to wait, wait, and wait for feedback from management, thinking, "I won't venture beyond where I am until I know how well I did."

Sometimes I am asked how soon scorecards should be set up for new employees. I tell them about Little League baseball. The first day the kids put on the uniform, they start tracking their batting average. They track every hitter and every fielder from the minute they step onto the field. Yet in business we frequently tell new employees to sit around for 90 days and then we'll get back to them. Too often all we measure is how they wear their hair, what they eat for lunch, or what time they like to go home. Tracking or scorekeeping must begin on day one.

Three Management Methods

There are three ways to manage a company—by observation, by judgment, or by measurement. When we manage by measurement, we keep score.

Observation management occurs when John, the sales manager, comes back from a tough sales appointment to find two of his sales representatives sitting on the table in the salesroom laughing and having a generally jolly time. What John doesn't know is that one of them has just lined up appointments with the executive officers of two companies John has been chasing for four years.

John doesn't know any of this, and having just been blown out on a sales presentation himself, he's not in a very good mood. As he walks by the salesroom he leans in and says, "Listen, if you two would get to work we wouldn't be in this sales slump."

Situations like that occur in companies all the time.

There are three basic problems with management by observation:

1. It is almost always inaccurate, like trying to judge a book by the cover, or a movie by the preview.

2. It is not relevant to what is going on. John observed two people sitting on a table having a good time. You can't capture all of the events in a single frame. It's like the cheerleader yelling at the referee for making the wrong call while the cheerleader's back was turned.

3. It is generally negative. There seems to be something in human nature that makes it easier to observe the negative than the positive. Had the two young salespeople been on the phone, John probably wouldn't have said anything. There's no way to win when you use observation management.

Management by judgment occurs when John walks by the salesroom a second time and the two salespeople are still sitting on the table gabbing. John is likely to make a judgment: "Kids today don't work as hard as I did when I broke into the business."

In some corporations you hear the nautical phrase "He can't get rid of his barnacles." That means the person made a mistake back in 1957 and everybody remembers it. Every time he looks as if he is getting close to that same kind of decision, they say, "Oh, yeah, you remember when he did that back in . . ." The danger with management by judgment is that too often generalizations are made from insufficient data.

When you have to correct someone, always be ultra-specific. Say, "You were 45 minutes late for that Tuesday afternoon appointment," rather than "How come you are always late?" Unfortunately most managers manage by judgment and observation rather than by measurement. Judgment leads to prejudgment, which leads to prejudice. Prejudice leads to blindness.

Too often people make negative generalizations—that's when somebody says on Monday morning that the economy is in tough shape and nobody is buying that day. Too often business-people let their thoughts about one or two negative events grow like a cancer.

"You always . . ."

"You never have . . ."

"You won't . . ."

Never make a negative generalization! Even if you think it is true, it will do more harm than good. Instead, when describing a negative situation always be ultra-specific. How much are sales down? How many calls did not get made? What specific behavior is it that you are concerned about? Don't make wandering generalities.

Management by measurement is the one management method that works. I believe that our progress in business, or life, relates directly to our ability to measure. Four hundred years ago the most portable mechanical timepiece you could have was a water clock on a wagon. It was ten feet high and weighed 300 pounds, and you had to pull it around with horses. And it didn't keep good time if the water slopped around. The smallest unit of distance measurement at that time was the distance from King Henry's thumb to his nose, a meter. Everything people built was designed around that unit of measurement.

Today we are much better at measuring things. We have memory chips and integrated circuits. Thousands of numbers can be sorted on a surface no larger than a pinhead. Without measuring and counting, such technology would not be possible. Quartz watches are all based on the frequency at which the quartz crystal vibrates. Our progress is based on our ability to improve measurement.

Management by measurement is relevant to the process being measured. The ability to sit on a table and carry on a friendly conversation with another salesperson is not relevant to sales success, though too much time sitting can certainly take time away from more productive activities.

So, *first, measurement is relevant to the process.* It tells you what happened, especially on the bottom line.

Second, measurement is usually exact. By that I mean when you measure something, you get the real numbers. You know where you stand. For example, if I asked you to sit down and create a financial statement, listing all your assets and liabilities, in most cases you'd discover you are better off financially than you thought you were. You are always better off when you know where you stand.

Third, exact measurements make work as enjoyable as play because participants have a way to win. When specific measurements are employed, it suddenly becomes possible for the employee to win.

You may be asking, if there are so many obvious benefits to maintaining exact measurements, why then is not more measuring going on? Perhaps some people think it is just too much trouble, or that it is too time consuming. Others may be afraid of the truth—suspecting they may not be doing a very good job. They don't think they are winning, so they don't want to know the score. What they don't realize is that they cannot win unless they keep score. There is no way to win without a score.

There are three kinds of workers or players.

1. Those who know they are winning.
2. Those who know they are losing.
3. Those who don't know the score.

It is a fact of life that those who keep score, whether they are winning or losing, win more over the long run. These are the people who accept personal responsibility for their own actions. They would rather know the score while losing than not know the score. The people who achieve financial independence do so by knowing the score. They are the people who set specific goals and keep track of progress toward those goals, even when things are not going smoothly.

I have never met a winner who didn't know the score. I have never met a professional golfer who didn't know who else was on the leader board. People play and modify their behavior based on the feedback of their progress against an acceptable standard—the scorecard.

The great tradition of Notre Dame football is reflected in a subtle fashion on the locker-room wall. You can't help but notice all the scores of the great Notre Dame victories over their great rivals emblazoned on those walls. The impact is awesome. *Winners keep track of results. Losers keep track of reasons.*

George Brett, the great .375-plus hitter for the Kansas City Royals, was once asked in an interview what his batting average was that day. This was during his quest for the second .400 season.

He said, "I've got 169 hits in 450 at bats. My batting average is .375, and if I go three for four today it will go to .379."

One of the reporters was astonished at Brett's command of mathematics and questioned him on it.

George said, "It's not very unusual. All the .350-plus hitters in the league can tell you what today's performance will mean to their overall batting averages."

But let a reporter ask any of the players batting under .200 what their averages are, and they'll say, "Oh, I'm not sure, a buck and some change," meaning somewhere over .100.

Winners like George Brett understand that there is no joy in victory without running the risk of defeat.

You cannot sit by as a spectator in the game of work. You must trade your season tickets for a pair of shoes and come down on the field, the only place where points can be scored.

Management by measurement is facing the truth, taking away the language and thinking of noncommitment. When you ask people if they have completed their work yet, and they say, "Basically," "Pretty much," or "Just about," that means they have accomplished somewhere around 20 percent of the goal. These verbal diversions are a way to run away from the truth. English teachers call them euphemisms.

Euphemisms, or escape words, are rampant in business. We use the phrase "pretty much" when we have no idea at all—"pretty close" when we haven't even started. When we haven't finished a job, we say we're "just about done." *Avoiding* euphemisms vastly improves the level of communications.

There is too much truth in exact measurement for some people. Losers don't have the courage to face the truth of exact measurement. They want to run away from the truth by focusing on activities instead of results. When exact measurements are made, things are brought into clear focus, and there is no place to hide.

If you have the courage to keep score, even when you are losing, you will win more in the long run. The elimination of uncertainty through scorekeeping increases the ability to take calculated risks.

The Cash-Flow Euphemism

One of the greatest rituals in America today takes place in the private clubs where business leaders meet to eat, exercise, and share problems with each other. When you walk into your club, somebody is likely to say, "How's business?"

You might respond, "Not bad. I just have a little cash-flow problem."

The person that asks the question, and everybody else, nod their heads knowingly like the great gods of Egypt and say, "Boy, we sure know what you mean. We're in the same situation."

What are these people saying? How can the problem not be bad if the cash won't flow, not even dribble a bit?

The *cash-flow problem* is a euphemism, a form of escapism, a way to avoid a serious business problem. *Cash flow is the barometer of business health.* Saying everything is fine except for cash flow is like saying the patient is fine except for a 105-degree temperature. Executives have to pull their heads out of the sand to face their problems and deal with them.

There's no such thing as a cash-flow problem. Cash-flow problems, as people call them, are symptoms of deeper problems.

Maybe the problem is not being able to collect the money owed you. It may be that you purchased too much inventory, or the wrong kind of inventory, and don't have the courage to liquidate the excess. Maybe you don't have the courage to raise prices and go out and sell value. Or you don't have the backbone to cut unnecessary overhead—you think you can't cut anybody back even though you have enough help to do fifty percent more business. Perhaps you are bleeding the business by taking more out of the business than it is earning.

On the other hand, if you walked into the athletic club and someone asked, "How's it going?" and you said, "Well, not too bad, except I've bought more inventory than I know what to do with. I'm afraid to collect what people owe me. I don't have the courage to raise prices and sell on value. I'm afraid to lay off some of the employees I don't need. I'm bleeding the business by taking out more money than it is earning. But basically, things aren't bad"—if you responded like that, everybody in the club would look at you and say, "Gosh, what a terrible manager you are. How dare you call yourself a member of this club!"

Hitler's propaganda minister, Joseph Goebbels, said that if a lie is repeated long enough and loud enough everybody will believe it. That's the way it is with cash flow. If we are smart, we will look past the cash-flow generality to the specific places where our cash flew when we thought it was going to flow.

Cash-flow problems originate from five major problems:

1. *Too much inventory and other nonliquid assets.* Inventory is not being turned over fast enough to justify the cost of holding and handling it.

2. *Overly-high receivables.* Receivables are not being collected fast enough. Perhaps credit policies have remained weak as we have moved into a time of tight cash. Our courage to collect is being dampened by our concern for additional business. Maybe we are operating on the false assumption that sales from people who won't pay are somehow beneficial to our company.

3. *Inadequate gross-profit percentages.* We are unwilling to demand the markup necessary to survive and even prosper when sales are down.

4. *Unwillingness to implement cost-cutting measures.* I never cease to be amazed at the number of people who think they can increase sales from, say, $5 to $7 million without increasing costs, and if sales drop from $5 to $3 million, who don't think they can decrease costs. When they started their business, sales were at $2 or $3 million with proportionate costs, but they think there is no way they can cut costs back when sales go into a slump.

I acknowledge the fact that some costs are irreversible without doing long-term damage to the organization—space, buildings, real estate—solidly fixed things that have ongoing costs. But it is imperative that we recognize that a building too full of people and inventory can drain off a lot of unnecessary cash. The goal is to find that optimum level of operation where we can achieve maximum profitability and productivity. We've got to be able to bite the bullet.

5. *Inappropriate compensation for the owner or key decision-makers.* Owners or managers who combine a decrease in profitability with an increase in personal compensation are contributing to their own demise. Good farmers don't eat the seed corn.

Too often in business we forget a valuable lesson learned so well on the athletic field—that we don't negotiate the value of points. When a team scores a touchdown on an interception or fluke play, we don't run over to the field judge and say, "That one is worth only four points." No, the team gets six points, regardless of how easy the touchdown might have been. Yet in business, too often we try to mask the truth with words. We need to return to a communication style that says, "They messed up," not "Their performance is substandard, a little below the absolute minimum required in order to identify and get the job done." We have to have the courage to communicate accurately, to get to the bottom line.

We have enjoyed the comfortable euphemism of "cash flow problems" long enough. If your cash flow has dried up—if it is simply a drip where it used to be a gusher—then look along the pipeline for the holes. Don't be content with the wandering generality that growth, that benevolent dragon, kindly gobbled up your cash and stripped away the profits. Growth is no good unless it is profitable and funded from earnings. Legitimate earnings always were and always will be the best indication of a healthy company.

Remember, there is no such thing as a cash flow problem by itself. A shortage of cash is the result of other problems that you can do something about by keeping score.

Scorekeeping Basics

Following are some of the basics of good scorekeeping.

1. *Scorekeeping must be simple and objective.* One beautiful day as I was approaching the 18th hole, a golfer hit a ball that bounced off a rock in a stream, hit a tree, dribbled through a sand trap, and finally rolled onto the green. The resident pro looked over at me and said, "It's a good thing the scorecard does not make you tell how—just how many." A basketball score does not tell you about lucky tip-ins or hard-fought rebounds. A football score doesn't tell you how many interceptions were made or about the dropped receptions that should have been caught. But the individual players who got the tips, blocks, interceptions, or fumble recoveries know exactly how many they got, not just for the game, but for the entire season, and for last year too. Keep it simple.

2. *Scorekeeping must be self administered.* A scorecard is most effective when it is kept and updated by the player, as in golf and tennis. That's why three people in a tent can handle all the scorekeeping responsibilities for 140 participants in a golf tournament, or why four people can handle all the record keeping for a tennis tournament with thousands of participants. Periodically managers make the mistake of having their secretaries draw all the graphs and charts, or they have computers print out the scores two or three days after the fact. Self-administered graphing and scorekeeping is best.

When people keep their own scorecards, they know whether they won or lost that day and also how much they improved, regardless of whether or not the coach had a bad day. The players will also correct any deficiencies in their scores before the cards are turned in. Our self-concept or self-image is based on what we know and can prove about ourselves.

3. *Scorekeeping must offer a comparison between current personal performance, past personal performance, and an accepted standard.* Golf would no longer be a favorite national pastime if the only opportunity for comparison was whether or not we could beat Johnny Miller's record-setting score in the U.S. Open.

Golf survives and thrives because it has a scorekeeping system that allows me, for example, to compare myself, an 18 handicapper, with myself. If I go to the golf course and break 90, I get very excited. I compare my performance to my own past performance as well as to what the pros are doing.

Marathoning has a similar scorekeeping system. How many people would fight and kick and scream to get into the Boston Marathon if the clock was turned off after getting the time for the first-place finisher in each category?

The success of a scorekeeping system in recreation depends upon how well it compares his current performance with his past performance and with the accepted national average. Too often in business we generate a scorekeeping system that tells how well we did only in comparison to an arbitrary, artificially imposed standard.

4. *Scorekeeping should be dynamic.* It should allow players to review their performance during the game. In your business, is your scorekeeping more like ice hockey or figure skating? With the availability of the microcomputer, almost every kind of business information can be immediately available. Businesses no longer have to wait until the end of the month to know how they are doing. They can know daily, even hourly. As in ice hockey, employees can know the score as the game is being played. Yet most businesses still have 12 accounting periods just like before World War II. You don't know what you did in March until the middle of April—too late to make any adjustments for March.

To sum up the principles discussed in this chapter, consider bowling-league competition. Have you ever seen a non-motivated bowler? Everybody knows how to keep score. They throw those balls, knock down pins, and jump up and down, and you get the impression they would do almost anything for the prize money.

Work is a lot like bowling, except there's a person called a supervisor who stands in front of the pins with a curtain. The supervisor can see the pins, but the bowler can't. The bowler throws the ball, hears something, and says, "How'd I do?"

The supervisor says, "Change your grip."

The bowler says, "But how did I do?"

The supervisor says, "Move your foot." The bowler changes his grip and moves his foot and throws another ball.

The bowler hears the pins fall and asks, "How am I doing?" The supervisor says, "Put some tape in the thumb hole."

"How am I doing?" repeats the persistent bowler.

"Don't worry about it. We've got a review coming up in six months. We'll let you know then."

How long would bowling remain a popular activity under these conditions? Not very long.

Comparing business to bowling, supervisors who believe in management by measurement don't hold a blanket in front of the pins while the team members are bowling. They allow the players to know exactly how many pins they knock down with each ball.

Implementing a Scorekeeping System

The measurement principles discussed in this book need to be introduced carefully into the workplace. There is almost always resistance to change, and managers or employees who in the past have focused their attention on activity can be intimidated into inactivity by the threat of disclosing performance they may feel is less than acceptable. The truth can be painful and frightening. Employees who are sold on management by measurement and want to get involved of their own free will and choice generally benefit the most from the measurement system.

Too many middle managers today feel impotent in their ability to manage, to talk, to create, to discipline, to go, to move, to build with people. Our traditional American management philosophy to manage by exception, to focus on problems, to put out fires, results in a reluctance to regularly compliment and praise. We talk about the things that are going wrong instead of the things that are going right. As a result, subordinates are depreciated with more emphasis on shortcomings than accomplishments.

A singing group by the name of Three Dog Night had a hit song in the '60s called "Celebrate" that needs to be the theme song for managers. We have taken the emotion out of our management style. And yet we all watch the NBA champs, the winners of the Stanley Cup in the champagne showers of celebration. IBM has developed a real corporate culture around their ability to celebrate beyond expectation the accomplishment of their goals. Scorekeeping exists primarily so that we know when to begin the party.

A good scorekeeping system allows the worker or manager to establish his own self-worth in the eyes of his peers, subordinates, and supervisors. Everybody becomes more accurately and justly rewarded, stroked, or chastised, based on accurate performance records or scorecards.

4

Feedback

When performance is measured, performance improves.
When performance is measured and reported back,
the rate of improvement accelerates.

—Thomas S. Monson

What do you think would happen if a head coach approached his team in the locker room before an NFL playoff game and handed the quarterback a piece of paper listing one hundred plays in sequence, saying, "These are the plays I want you guys to execute, in the exact order listed on the paper."

Do you think any of the players would object? Of course they would, all of them. They'd think the coach was insane. Why?

In order for the best possible play to be called in any given situation, it is imperative that the person calling the play have feedback from the last play, or the last several plays—how many yards gained, which lineman is getting eaten up at the line of scrimmage, direction of the wind, which receivers are being left open and which ones are getting double coverage, how many yards remain for a first down or a touchdown, and so on. All this feedback is necessary in order to make the best possible call. Handing a team a predetermined list of plays before the opening kickoff eliminates the use of feedback in calling each play as it is executed. Nobody would be surprised to find out that a team not using feedback would have trouble winning in the NFL, NCAA, or even high school.

Yet how often in business is an employee handed a job description, or a predetermined set of plays, then expected to perform without continuing feedback? It happens more often than most businesses would like to admit. Feedback is as vital in business and in life in general as in athletics.

When a spouse returns from the hair stylist and says, "How do you like my haircut?" he or she is looking for feedback. The child who has just completed a project in his or her father's shop or just finished a first attempt at mowing the lawn is always interested in an opinion from a respected peer or superior.

In athletics feedback is more clearly acknowledged and more frequent than in business. When feedback suddenly becomes available in a business situation where it has not been available before, the results can be very dramatic.

I was called on to consult with a package express company a few years ago. They were concerned, among other things, about the filing of freight bills. They are a federally controlled company, and everything has to be filed for possible audits. They file millions of items every year. Their concern was that the four people doing the filing had been three days behind for thirty-six years, the entire time the company had been in business. The day they opened the door, the filing was three days behind and they had never been able to catch up.

"If you can't measure it, you can't manage it," I said to the supervisor of the people who did the filing.

You can guess her response. "We're too busy filing them to count them."

One of the vice presidents with me suggested that the filing could be measured by weighing the stacks of material to be filed. He thought this might work because each piece was the same size and therefore the same weight. Sounded like a good idea to me, but the supervisor said, "That's the second dumb idea I've heard today."

Finally we told her we were going to try it anyway. We came up with a measurement system similar to the golf handicap. We decided to monitor ounces per person-hour.

"I don't need that stuff," said the supervisor. "My people

work just as hard as anybody else in this company—all the time, every day."

"How do you know that?" I asked.

"I've got four file baskets," she said. "Every morning when I get here I spread the filing out equally into four file baskets and hand one to each file clerk, so the baskets are all even."

"What do you do on a heavy day?"

She looked at me as if I were a dummy, and she said, "Then the baskets are fuller." It was obvious at this point that this woman didn't want to be fooled with, but I persisted, telling her I wanted her to weigh the amount of filing going through the department. She didn't want to do it, but she finally agreed to weigh how much each person filed each day.

The first week we came up with an average of twenty-two ounces per person-hour. We didn't really know if that was good or bad, but it was a start. The next week we developed a score-card for the workers and taught them how to keep score as if we were teaching them a game. They recorded their own ounces per person-hour.

An interesting thing happened. The group average for the second week increased to thirty-three ounces per person-hour. And by the end of that week they were only one day behind—the first time in thirty-six years. We were witnessing a miracle.

The supervisor came to me and said, "Listen, I can't go any faster and be accurate."

"I understand that," I said. "That's all right. Don't worry about it."

The next week production increased to forty-five ounces per person-hour. There was no monetary incentive, no threatened disciplinary measures, no promised promotions. The only difference was that they were measuring performance, keeping score. Not only was the department no longer behind, but they were finishing each day's filing by 2 p.m. By the fourth week, production had increased to fifty-four ounces per person-hour and the filing was finished each day by 11:30 a.m.

I remembered when the supervisor was doing twenty-two ounces per hour and telling me she couldn't go any faster. The last time I checked she was up to seventy-two ounces per hour and still increasing. The big payoff was that the four people doing the filing were part of an eight-person work force in that department. When two of the non-file clerks needed to quit, the file clerks came to their supervisor and said, "Listen, if you'll tell us how to measure what they've been doing, we'll just pick it up."

The executive toy mail-order catalogs sell all kinds of computerized measuring machines. A recent ad was pushing a $39 pulse meter that goes on the end of your finger while you're jogging. It tells you whether you're living or dying. They've got a $199 radar gun that measures the speed of a baseball in midair. The ad says that if you measure your son or daughter's baseball pitch, the kid will learn to throw the ball faster. The same machine can be mounted on a tripod to measure your tennis serve. These machines are built and sold because the manufacturers and customers understand that when performance is measured and reported back the rate of improvement accelerates.

Probably the most significant achievement in biofeedback involves the heart. If patients can hear their heartbeat through a speaker system and see the screen on the cardiogram machine, the patients can actually learn to speed up or slow down their own heart. Feedback makes that possible.

Effective feedback is accompanied by its own set of terms, and the most important term is the *Results to Resource Ratio*—how much is being accomplished with the resources available—like the ounces per person-hour in the filing example. Successful managers have the capability of generating a greater result with the same amount of resource, or the same result with less resource. If they cannot measure it, they simply cannot do it, at least not on a regular, planned basis.

Sometimes we hear about coaches who have talented players but cannot produce a winning team. They are not able to manage their resources to produce results, and they are eventually fired.

All managers, whether they manage many people or just themselves, must make a list of all resources available to them—budget, person-hours, computer time, inventory, supplies, and so on. When you get right down to it, managers are people who turn resources into results. And the more efficiently they can do it, the more successful they are as managers. The Results to Resource Ratio can be used at every level of performance.

You can only chop down a forest one tree at a time. Let the accountants figure the return on investment ratios. This book deals with the micro-measurements, like the ounces per person-hour in the filing example, like Lee Nelson's minutes per bin of bottles described in the introduction. When all the micro-measurements are in place, the macro-measurements will take care of themselves.

You might be thinking, "Well that was a great story about the filing company, but what I do cannot be measured like that." You'd be surprised at what can be measured, even on the human side of a business. One time I went into an organization that sold building materials. They'd been on hard times for a few years along with the rest of the building industry.

They came up with a macro problem, wanting to know what they could do about their labor costs (resource) relative to sales (results). I told them we had to find a micro-indicator measuring results to resources. It didn't have to have the same scientific accuracy the tax people demand, just something to measure change over a period of time.

First we looked at what they produced. Sales. Dollars. But who knows what's happening to the dollar with its value changing almost daily. We finally determined that we could measure the number of invoices generated by the company. Then we looked at the resource that produces invoices—person-hours.

We went back over the last eighteen months of records, including thirty-nine pay periods, and figured out the number of person-hours per invoice for each pay period. The relationship of human resource to invoice output ranged from as high as 3.7 person-hours per invoice to a low of 1.9 for a two-week pay period—a significant variation.

As we analyzed the ratios, we discovered that the 1.9 ratio occurred when business peaked during the busy summer months. The higher ratios occurred during the slow off-season. Earlier, the company had suspected they were labor heavy during the winter months, but they weren't sure how much until we started tracking the person-hours per invoice. With the confidence of exact measurement, management decided they never needed more than 2.25 person-hours per invoice, even during the slack periods.

Now, all this may not sound very sophisticated to the experienced business manager, but that company processed an average of sixteen hundred invoices per pay period. The company was able to cut out almost two thousand person-hours per pay period. So who is going to do the work? The people who are left, and they are going to do exactly what they have always done. The labor that was removed was expendable, unnecessary, but the company didn't know it until the micro Results to Resource Ratio was developed. In dealing with the human resource, managers must realize that it is flexible and can be managed to do what they want it to do. But it cannot be managed unless it is measured.

Coonradt Feedback Corollaries

Through the years I have found two corollaries that expand on Thomas Monson's statement: "When performance is measured, performance improves. When performance is measured and reported back, the rate of improvement accelerates."

1. *Increasing the frequency of feedback improves the quality and quantity of performance.* If you're having a difficult time managing your labor resource and you're measuring it monthly, then go to a weekly measurement. It will improve. If you go to a daily measurement, it will improve again. And if you go to an hourly measurement, it may improve even more.

You may think it will take too much time to administer all these measurements, Meaningful measurement takes no time at all. In the example of the file clerks and in example after example we see that the small amount of time it takes to count results is minuscule when compared with the improved results.

2. *When feedback is illustrated on charts and graphs, the impact is even greater.* In business today we have tremendous

amounts of data. It comes in stacks and boxes, making us wonder if the programmers think they are being paid for the pounds of paper they run through the printers. But data by itself is of little value. It must become useful management knowledge that can be used to make decisions. Graphs and charts make this possible by making information easier to understand and digest. In other words, the feedback—the "score"—becomes even more clear because it is graphically displayed, thus ensuring even better performance.

Remember, in the absence of clearly defined goals and accurate scorekeeping, we are forced to concentrate on activity and ultimately become enslaved by it. The goal of every business must be to get to the point where everybody on the team has an individual scorecard. Without clearly defined goals and precise scorekeeping, workers will continue to pay for the privilege of working harder than they work when they are paid.

Is timely feedback important? Is frequent feedback important? In the 1984 Summer Olympics, Julie Ann McNamara, one of our great gymnasts, did a routine, and there was some momentary concern about her score. The numbers didn't come up when they were supposed to. There was a ninety-second delay, and during that ninety seconds, you could feel the trauma travel throughout Pauley Pavilion's sixteen thousand spectators and then around the world over the airwaves.

What was wrong? Where was the concern? Ninety seconds, and the world was wondering if the Olympics would go on. And yet how often do we put off giving employees feedback on their performance? Do we avoid it because we don't like confrontation? Are we unwilling to sit down and explain what we need to have done, what the employees are doing right, and what they need to do to improve? Sometimes we put it off and put it off and finally walk up and say, "I've decided to give you twenty-five more dollars a week; be happy with that and go home." We need to do better than that.

If you don't think feedback is important, try telling your spouse just once that the outfit he or she has selected for a big evening is just "okay."

5

Choice

I'm a downhill skier. I think that walking up a mountain with a perfectly good ski lift on it is crazy, but my skinny-ski friends, the cross-country skiers, say, "Why pay somebody to haul you up a mountain that you can walk up on your own two legs?" I also think that jumping out of an airplane while the engine is still turning is absolutely crazy, but the sky divers think it's great fun; and, of course, as a certified scuba diver, I think it makes perfect sense to strap forty minutes of air on my back and then go two hundred feet from my next breath of fresh air just to get the glory of the depths. But that's choice.

Choice is what drives America. Look around your neighborhood at the various models of cars that are being driven. Look at the options. In the People's Republic of China, they have very few cars, and all the cars are the same. But here we have a choice. We have over forty different brands of skis in any length we want, manufactured all around the world. We have over twenty major golf-club manufacturers. Choice is what America is all about. It is the basis of our Declaration of Independence. It is the basis of our Constitution. We will spill American blood on foreign soil in order to defend our right to vote, just so half of us can stay home every election. But if you try to take that right, that choice, away from us, we will fight to the death to retain it.

In spite of our freedom of choice, numerous surveys show that two-thirds of American workers are unhappy with their jobs. They don't always know what they would rather do, but they are unhappy with their alternatives.

Come with me at 7:30 in the morning to that major freeway leading into town. Let's post a sign that says, "If you have to go to work, turn on your lights. If you want to go to work, honk your horn." What are we going to wind up with? The quietest light show you ever saw. Come with me on that same freeway on the way home just before the Memorial Day weekend. Let's post a sign that says, "If you have to go boating, turn on your lights. If you want to go boating, honk your horn." The noise would be deafening.

Our lives are comprised completely of have-tos and want-tos. We enjoy the things we want to do; the things we have to do, we are usually not too excited about. Why is it that so many Americans do not enjoy their jobs? Because in their work, their choices are usually severely limited. They are told exactly what to do and *how* to do it. They don't have very much fun. And they don't perform as well as if they were having fun.

In *A Passion for Excellence*, Tom Peters and Nancy Austin describe the freedom of choice at W. L. Gore and Associates, Inc. When new employees come on board, they aren't *given* an assignment. They are allowed to wander around for a few weeks and *find* an assignment. "We organize ourselves around voluntary commitments," says Gore. I once had an opportunity to meet one of Gore's associates while on a business trip. I asked her if they really operate in that fashion. She said, "That's exactly the way we run it."

In recreation, people can choose to do what they excel at. As a result, they succeed. If they want to play golf, they can play golf. If they want to play tennis, they can play tennis. How many times have you heard someone say, "Well, I have to go play tennis today"? I'm a tennis player—by choice. But racquetball players don't think I get any exercise, and a handball player I once knew said, "A real man doesn't need a racquet to beat up on a little bitty ball."

The greatest tennis players in the world may not make very good golfers, but nobody is forcing them to play golf. The same principle holds true in business; the more choices you give your employees—within the bounds of your business, of course—the better they will perform, and the more they will enjoy it.

If you give your players more freedom, a few may decide to do just enough to get by. Of course, that's probably all they are doing with the freedom they have now. But many of your players will do more and achieve more than you ever dreamed possible. Why? Because most people become committed to what they freely choose. People need to own their jobs, and they can own them only if they have a choice about what their jobs are, about what their goals are, and about how they will reach those goals.

Winners don't seek to change the rules; they only seek to understand them well enough to win. So is it with choice. You must recognize which choices are yours to make and which ones you can't worry about.

I now realize that in my athletic career if I could have changed the stickiness of a football at the moment it was being thrown to me in a crowded stadium, then I would have been All Pro, without a doubt. Because there have been times in a stadium, when I was open, that the quarterback delivered it into my hands, and I could have caught it if the thing had been just a little stickier. I had no choice about that, but I did have a choice on how to cut on that defensive back. I had choices on my technique, whether to punt cross-handed or with an over-hand grip. I had choices in my methods.

And in the workplace, if you will trust your people to make the choices that they can make, they will become winners. To important people, we always explain why. To unimportant people, we simply tell how. People can tell how we feel about them by the way we talk to them. Important people are allowed to make choices. Unimportant people have their choices restricted. What you need to look at is what you are communicating about your players based on the choices you allow them to make.

Workers need to understand the reasons behind the things you ask them to do. They need to help negotiate the results that are expected. They need to be allowed to help determine what the company will become, because when they go home and talk to their neighbors, they are their company, and they need to have a choice about what they are. Finally, after all these things have been settled, people need to be allowed to use whatever methods they are comfortable with to bring the goals to pass.

If people had always insisted on doing things the way their predecessors did, we would have none of the progress we have had, but progress has come from those people who were willing to think outside the usual limits, even with their eyes clearly on the goal, and who have figured out better, different, and faster ways to do things.

Decision-Making

People who can make good decisions are some of the most sought after people in American business. We celebrate decision makers. We want to have them in our companies. But if we're not willing to advance the challenge of choice to beginning players, from the day they come in the door, about where their desks sit, about how their offices are decorated, about all of the things that give them a sense of ownership and don't detract at all from the long-term success of the company, we can't build the decision makers of tomorrow.

Are you encouraging choice? Are you asking for innovation? Do you make clear what things in your company can't be changed and in what things workers are free to choose?

Behavior

Our choices *are* our behavior, and we cannot change the result without changing the behavior. That's a frightening lesson for many of us to learn, but a true one. I cannot get consequence B by behaving in way A. "I would like to lose weight as long as I don't have to give up the hot fudge." "I want to be financially independent but I can't give up my credit cards." "I'd like to be a marathon runner, but don't ask me to run in the rain." "I'd like to compete in downhill skiing, but I don't want to take lessons."

There's no way to get around the fact that behavior precedes results. As the behavior of players determines the team results, so does the behavior of workers and managers determine the success of a business. Too often businesses try to blame outside influences if they don't get desired results, when it's the way the players behave that determines whether or not the team wins with any degree of consistency.

We can go one step further: Attitude is the prime cause of behavior.

Attitude

The way I *think* determines the way I will *act*, whether it be in a momentary fit of rage or in contemplation in a planning session. It is imperative to understand that the thought precedes the act. Also, it is impossible to behave *consistently* contrary to a basic attitude. We may behave contrary to our values at times, by coercion or inducement, but not consistently.

This brings us to a problem facing most coaches. They may be able to specify what behavior is required in a player to produce the desired result, but they don't know how to mold the attitude so the desired behavior can be achieved.

There are two powerful forces that form attitudes. One is a significant emotional event. The death of a loved one while participating in a sport may significantly shape our attitude toward that sport. A severe reprimand from the first boss may shape a worker's attitude toward management for years to come. Significant emotional events, while necessary and recognized attitude modifiers, are not easily duplicated in coaching environments. They are difficult to control.

The second formative force in attitude is conditioning. Conditioning is the same force that trains the dog with the electric collar or makes Pavlov's dogs salivate when the bell is rung.

Conditioning

You don't have an electric collar, but you must admit that your past conditioning influences the way you act. You may have been reared with these statements:

"Children should be seen and not heard."

"Never bite off more than you can chew."

"Never speak unless spoken to."

"Never go where you're not wanted."

"Never talk to strangers."

If you're in a marketing role, your entire job description is contrary to the great parental advice that kept you safely out of the clutches of kidnappers on your way to school. The cornerstone of sales call reluctance in the American sales force was planted there on those sidewalks to kindergarten.

If you don't believe me, walk into the nearest elevator and recognize that it's a six-by-eight-foot American institution where fourteen strangers can stand close enough to touch each other and nobody talks. We all duck in, turn around, and look at the numbers above the door.

The next time you get into an elevator, do not turn around. Simply face your fellow passengers. Watch their eyes go to the floor. And if you feel bold, say, "Good morning, how are you?" Conditioning does shape attitudes.

What makes conditioning such a powerful force? Repetition. Spaced repetition. We did not learn to avoid strangers because we were told once, but because most of us were told every time we left the house to be wary of strangers. Perhaps all of our parents went to school together and learned to say the same things to their children. None of us were brash enough to turn around as we left the house and wonder what our other choices were. It did not occur to us to question the source of that information. But today, how many of our investment philosophies or management decisions are guided by those youthful admonitions?

Today, how many of us "look before we leap," "save our money for a rainy day," and "make sure that if we can't say something nice about somebody we don't say anything at all"?

This last one has had a great impact on restricting management discipline.

Spaced Repetition

When you are coaching you must understand that success is the result of behavior, which is determined by attitudes, which are formed by conditioning, which takes place through spaced repetition.

Repetitive learning is the only vehicle to modify conditioning, which alters the attitudes that control our behavior, which produces the results we want. One trip, one lecture, one seminar, one tape won't do it. Advertisers say it takes eight repetitions before the consumer will even notice your product.

Winners understand the importance of conditioning as it relates to attitudes, behavior, and eventually achieving success or results. Winners are constantly conditioning themselves by reviewing their written goals, reading good books, surrounding themselves with other goal-oriented individuals, and inviting spaced repetition of positive thoughts while pushing negative thoughts out of their minds.

You can bet the Washington Redskins don't make up very many plays during the course of a game. The bread-and-butter plays of their offense have been rehearsed in practice dozens, if not hundreds, of times. The players are conditioned by repetition to respond in a predetermined way to each play number.

Winners in business also understand the conditioning process, the need for spaced repetition, and do everything in their power to use this powerful force to achieve success and results.

Spaced repetition influences our conditioning. Our conditioning influences our attitudes. And our attitudes influence our behavior—the things we choose to do. Thus, we can directly influence ourselves and our people to make the choices that will bring success.

I once consulted with a company that built modular housing. The carpenters worked inside a factory. We had been tracking the total square footage produced by the workers, and it totaled about

44,000 square feet of finished housing in five days. It was the week of the deer hunt, and some of the supervisors went to the vice president of manufacturing and said, "We would like to get off work early Friday." The vice president said, "If you get 44,000 square feet done by Friday at noon, you can leave then." I suggested that we should see what would happen if we allowed the workers to choose the day they could get off work as long as the 44,000 feet of work was finished. The vice-president took my suggestion, and the workers did leave work early—at 2:00 on Wednesday. The plumbers and the electricians and the roofers all helped each other, and the work was done in record time. Why? Because they had a choice. Before that they had to work until Friday at 5:00. They *had* to. But when they had the opportunity to do what they *wanted* to do, they were willing to do it.

If you want to motivate your workers, if you want them to feel like members of the team, if you want them to work as if the company belonged to them, you must give them the freedom to choose the way to succeed. If you do, they will come through for you—beyond your wildest dreams.

6

Field of Play

Great managers constantly seek to minimize uncertainty.

—Chuck Coonradt

Who could forget Rosie Ruiz in the Boston Marathon. She finished first among the female contestants. Her time, compared to her past performances, was unbelievably good. Why? Because outside the field of play, outside the rules of competition, she had hopped onto a bus, which, of course, greatly improved her time. She had finished the race, but her performance was not within the criteria established by those who controlled the race. Her time was not recorded in the record book, and there is no Boston Marathon bus-ride trophy. The Boston Marathon has a clearly defined field of play, and Rosie got herself into trouble by trying to perform outside the field of play.

In organizations of every kind, we hear the cry to improve communication. Improving communication is the top of millions of conversations every day. This problem isn't nearly as serious on the playing field among athletes as it is in business. How many of the sixty or so plays in a football game are not communicated to the players? Very few, if any.

People keep trying to solve communication problems. We've seen the era of transactional analysis. We've gone through sensitivity training and empathy building and role playing. We've had the job description writers, and I must admit an incredible bias against their efforts—mainly because of their lack of specificity and the necessity of the Supreme Court to interpret the language of many job descriptions. A client of mine, a president of a company generating net profits in the millions, had a fourteen page job description, and the only numbers contained therein were the page numbers. It's very difficult to understand success and failure, winning and losing, good and bad, in that morass of confusion.

Before we develop our goals, we must establish certain criteria about our field of play. When Dr. James Naismith hung that first peach basket up on the barn wall and started the game of basketball, he had to define the dimensions of the field of play. He had to set the rules. He had to identify to the players when their baskets would count and when they would not, where they could dribble and where they would be out of bounds. And when Abner Doubleday organized the sport of baseball, the primary improvement he brought to the previous activities of throwing rocks at squirrels and hitting chestnuts with sticks was the design and dimension of the field of play.

If you were given several acres of raw ground and given the assignment to lay it out for a sports center, one of your design techniques might be to take scale models of the various fields of play and begin arranging them on that property in order to make the best use of space. It would make no sense to stick a basketball standard here, a hockey goal there, and a baseball backstop over here without knowing implications of the decision.

You can't go out and start playing until your field of play is clearly and completely established. The boundaries must be in place before you can set the goals and begin to play the game. Even in a casual game of touch football or sand-lot baseball, the kids will decide the boundaries before they start playing.

In sports, fields of play are so well known as to be almost taken for granted. If I say, "Let's go play tennis," you correctly assume that we're going to a tennis court. If I say, "Grab your golf clubs," your only question is which course we are going to play on.

55

The shape of the field says so much about the nature of the game that it is incredible to me that we have not done a better job in business in defining the field of play before we just run off with a station wagon loaded with equipment or drop a new personal computer on a manager's desk.

Our problem, I think, lies in the fact that in recreation the fields of play exist already. They've always just been there. So we walk onto them and accept the assumptions they give us without really thinking about them. We've never had to create fields of play, and we have not been taught how to do it.

What shape is the field of play in basketball? A rectangle. What is a tennis court? Again a rectangle. A football field is a rectangle, too. What shape is a race track? Oval. A baseball diamond is not a diamond, but actually a square, and if you look at the entire field you find a quarter of a circle. We couldn't play any of these games without first accepting the standard field of play. What do you think would be the reaction at the New York City Athletic Club if an unknown college running back walked in the door and announced that he had come for the Heisman Trophy?

"But I rushed over three thousand yards this year!" claims the player as he is led to the exit.

"We don't have any record of that."

"Ask the coach. He saw me. I did it during practice."

"But that doesn't count."

The point here is that if you are going to play a game, you've got to know where the out-of-bounds markers are. You must have a general overview of the field of competition. You can't take credit for performance outside your assigned area.

You may be wondering why I even bother to discuss such an obvious principle. I do so because you can find hundreds of business examples—common, everyday occurrences—where people are expected to perform without knowing the field of play. Our ability to overlook the obvious is incredible.

Fields of Play in Business

Consider the employee who has just come out of a retail staff meeting where he has been chewed out for allowing excessive customer returns.

"We took back a thirty-five-dollar gadget yesterday that was purchased almost a year ago," scolded the manager. "How can we expect to make money when employees are that ignorant of company policy?"

Two hours later the employee is unknowingly waiting on a good friend of the manager who wants to return something that wasn't purchased in the store. The manager knows she is a very good customer. The employee knows what he heard in the morning meeting. The manager and the employee have different perceptions of the field of play, which has never been clearly defined.

As the employee courteously explains to the customer why the company cannot accept the returned merchandise, the manager walks up and says, "Good morning, Mrs. Fishburg. How are you? Glad to have you in our store today. Of course we'll take your return."

The employee is suddenly confused. The field of play is no longer clear, and for the rest of the day that employee would just as soon hide in a corner. You cannot change the rules in the middle of the game without destroying the self-confidence of the player.

Can you remember a situation in your business where someone overstepped their bounds, played outside their sandbox, messed up someone else's job because they didn't have a clear understanding of their field of play? You can probably think of lots of examples.

Can you think of anyone in business with a clearly defined field of play? Someone who works in an environment of absolute certainty with clear policies and procedures? Clear work rules, security, guarantees, a certain amount of vacation, a person who knows exactly what to do every day? You might have in mind someone who works on an assembly line or perhaps runs a mail sorting machine at the post office. You may think people with such jobs are not happy because they are not challenged. They don't have the variety, fun, and risk that you might have, but they do have a high comfort level, a very high degree of certainty.

In such cases, people have a field of play that is similar to a square. A square is symmetrical, and the sides are a certain length. Nobody has any question about what its boundaries are. In business, freedom is greatest when boundaries are clearly defined. When I know exactly where the edge is, I am more confident. I would rather be following a police officer in his car than be concerned about him hiding with his radar gun. I would rather drive on a treacherous patch of icy road when I have clear vision than I would when I'm in the fog. My freedom and security are greatest when my boundaries are clearly defined.

I was driving with a broken speedometer cable to a city thirty miles north of my home one day. I was late for an appointment, and I'd received two speeding tickets in the previous ninety days; one more and they would take away my driver's license. The uncertainty was incredible.

I'd look at my watch and be reminded that I was running late. I would speed up. Then, realizing I was passing other cars, I figured I was going too fast and would slow down. Every time I came over a hill, I fully expected to see a highway patrol car with a radar gun waiting for me. Gradually the uncertainty forced me to restrict my performance, to shrink back. Since I didn't know where the boundaries were, I had to restrict my performance in an effort to avoid going out of bounds. With two speeding tickets already, I simply couldn't take that risk. Had my speedometer been working, I could have moved comfortably to the very edge of the boundary at fifty-five miles an hour without any anxiety, knowing I was within the field of play.

Sometimes we find ourselves in a field of play shaped like a doughnut. We have a large area of responsibility and a small area of authority. This is the frustration of many people in administrative roles or staff positions who are given broad parameters of what line management expects but little authority to carry out those expectations. Their response is to wander about the company saying, "Charlie told me . . . ," "Charlie says . . . ," "Charlie wants us to . . . ," and they are never really sure about the authority they represent and can find no satisfaction in their own authority. The doughnut, unfortunately, becomes a center where very little is accomplished, where people "dough-not" do anything.

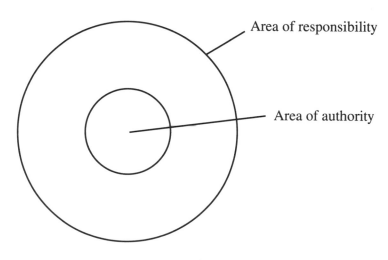

Area of responsibility

Area of authority

In the early days of home computers there was a mad rush into the field, with dozens of companies competing vigorously for market share. Rebates and price cutting were the common fare as manufacturers pushed their wares on confused retailers. The result was an oversupply of home computers, resulting in downward price pressure. Most of these aggressive computer manufacturers not only found themselves without profit but in a struggle for survival. No one bothered to set the boundaries before they started to play the game. Market sizes, demographics, buying patterns, and customer profiles were not clearly defined. Without a clear field of play, the result was chaos.

Another common field of play in business is shaped like an amoeba—a random, globular shape. It describes the employee's understanding of what he or she thinks is expected, and the only problem is that it wiggles and jiggles and changes shape. When something goes wrong that the employee didn't think was his or her responsibility, sure enough, someone points it out as his or her responsibility on the amoeba.

Point the player thought was safe. Amoeba has ability to change shape to make the player accountable if anything goes wrong.

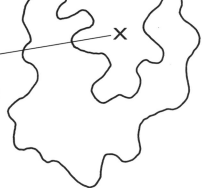

As mentioned earlier, the ideal field of play may be represented by a square. The only real problem with the square is that it has a lid. If we were to take the lid off the square and provide a growth outlet, then I believe we would have an ideal field of play for business, as in the diagram on the next page.

Field of Play

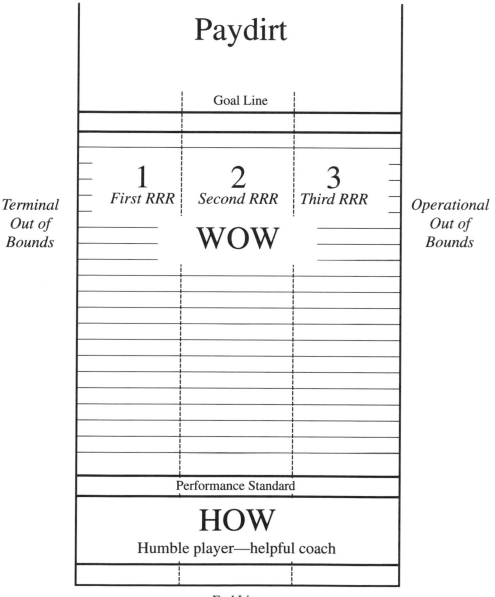

Paydirt

Goal Line

	1	2	3	
Terminal Out of Bounds	*First RRR*	*Second RRR*	*Third RRR*	*Operational Out of Bounds*

WOW

Performance Standard

HOW

Humble player—helpful coach

End Line

Performance Out of Bounds

On the left side of the field of play are the terminal out of bounds—those things that, if players did them, they would immediately be fired, such as embezzling company funds. On the right side are the operational out of bounds—things that players are not allowed to do while working, such as wearing a T-shirt and jeans to a sales presentation. They would not be fired, but they might be sent home to change. At the bottom of the field is the performance out of bounds—the area where the employees are simply not performing. The players may not be removed from the team, but they may be transferred to a new area of responsibility.

The HOW is really the first word in the coaching statement "How can I help?" Meaning, that the coach is ready to give his or her full attention and experience to helping the player select a course of action (plays) which will return their performance to above the performance standard. In this area, the players are expected to be humble, to accept the guidance of the coach. And the coach is expected to be helpful, to do what he or she can to get the player to meet the minimum standard.

WOW means exactly that. The coach is the cheerleader. Giving positive reinforcement for results above the performance standard. Players with results in this area are given great freedom. This is the area where the players are performing above the minimum accepted standard. Here, they are given great freedom to play the game however they wish within the rules to achieve the goals they have set. They are not subject to close scrutiny or oversupervision, although they may use the coach as a resource as needed.

The areas marked 1, 2, and 3 are the three Results to Resources Ratios for which the players are responsible. Your employees may have only one, or they may have more. This is up to you and them.

Across the goal line is the paydirt, where the players receive those special levels of compensation or privileges that are reserved for those who turn in superlative performances.

You should sit down with every one of your employees and with every new employee that joins your team and define with them these elements on their field of play, especially as the field of play may differ for every employee.

The first thing you should define is what constitutes terminal and operational out of bounds.

One time I was working with a fast-food company that had seven outlets. In the middle of a discussion of fear and expectations, I turned to one of the managers and said, "Dave, do you have any fear in this company?" and he said,

"Oh, we've got a bunch of it."

"What are you afraid of?" I asked.

"I'm afraid of being fired."

It got rather hushed in the room because the owner and president was there with the supervisory staff and administrative people. I was prompted to ask, "Dave, since you're afraid of being fired, tell me one thing that you know if you were doing, you'd be gone."

He thought for a moment and then said, "I don't know."

Think about it. *A person in almost constant fear who did not know what would get him fired.*

It seemed like a good idea to persist in the questioning. I asked the same question of the next manager and received the same response. All the managers had the same fear. I take my hat off to the president and owner of that company, who sat silently, taking a rather bitter pill. As I met with him later in an individual conference, he relayed his astonishment that he had not been more aware of his managers' fear of losing their jobs. I assured him that his situation was not unusual and suggested that we correct it by listing the things he felt were serious enough to justify terminating a relationship.

At the next meeting with the managers, the eighteen-point list was passed around. The room was silent as the managers read the list with great interest. Then, one by one, sighs began to come forth from each of the participants, and David, our first manager, summed it up far better, I think, than anyone else when he said, "But I'm not doing any of these things."

To which the president responded. "Then, David, you have nothing to worry about."

At The Game of Work, LLC, we establish what constitutes the terminal and operational out of bounds in the Game of Work with our *out-of-bounds statement*, which is reproduced below. In this statement, we spell out exactly what will cause a player to be fired, and we make no apologies about it. If employees don't like these conditions, they are free to seek employment elsewhere. And if they agree to these conditions, they are free from worry about what might cause them to lose their job. They already *know* what might cause them to lose it, so they can then concentrate on winning within the rules and without fear.

After you have explained to the players what constitutes out of bounds, you must define with them the other areas on the field of play. At The Game of Work, LLC, we do this in writing with our *field of play development agenda* and our *field of play coaching meetings agenda*. By reading through these agendas and their supporting documents (which are also reproduced here), you will be able to get a good idea of how we define the fields of play in our organization. Then you may want to take a similar course in yours, using our documents (which are also reproduced here), you will be able to get a good idea of how we define the fields of play in our organization. Then you may want to take a similar course in yours, using our documents as models. We bind the documents together with a cover page, and we call this collection of documents our *field of play agreement*. It allows us to make clear to our workers exactly what is expected of them.

How you define the field of play to your players is not really important. But what is important is that you *do* define it accurately and clearly in a way that works for your organization.

The Game of Work, LLC

Field of Play
Out of Bounds

Terminal Out of Bounds

Because our business is built on trust and respect for our integrity and professionalism, we must be above reproach. Therefore, those things which will result in a member of G.O.W., LLC Being subject to immediate termination of employment if engaged in are:

1. Embezzlement or theft; any misappropriation of money due to G.O.W., LLC; misappropriations of supplies, inventories, or trade secrets.

2. Any violation of copyrights held by G.O.W., LLC, its principals, or any other supplier of material which may result in endangering our agreements.

3. Failure to perform a service for which we have been contracted or been paid.

4. Using G.O.W., LLC representation or the contacts you have made as a result of your employment or developed expertise to perform any service like or similar to our services which is not billed through the company.

5. Lying or any misrepresentation of the facts concerning status of a sale, an account receivable, or the whereabouts or behavior of self or a fellow employee.

6. Any adultery or fornication or immoral relationship with a G.O.W., LLC Employee, or an employee of any of our client companies.

7. Disorderly behavior which is alcohol or drug induced in the presence of a client, whether you are working or socializing, or are observed by the client.

8. Any declaration to another individual(s) which is disloyal, degrading, or defamatory of the company, its officers, or its employees.

9. Failure to treat any employee, client employee, or client as an individual and member of the species created above all.

10. Any behavior, public or private, which detracts from the ethical and professional reputation of The Game of Work, LLC.

Operational Out of Bounds

1. Failure to attend two consecutive regularly scheduled training meetings without approval from the sales manager or officer of The Game of Work, LLC.

Read and Received: _____

Approved: _____

Signed: _____

The Game of Work, LLC

Field of Play
Development Agenda

Recommendations

1. Compile a field of play folder for each agreement (1 copy each to coach and player). The folder contains:

    A. Field of player diagram [see p. 61].

B. Out of bounds statements—terminal and operational [see pp. 66].

C. Expectancy statements from player and coach [see p. 71].

D. Support commitments to player from coach.

E. 3-5 scorecards on areas of measurable performance.

2. All meetings must be completed in no more than four weeks.

3. Each team member negotiates his/her agreement as a player before initiating any agreements as a coach.

First Meeting

Date Completed

_____ 1. Coach establishes written out of bounds.
        A. *Terminal.*
            1. Company-wide.
            2. Individual applications.

        B. *Operational.*

_____ 2. Coach suggests 3-5 areas for scorekeeping (sales per day, average order, gross profit per transaction).

_____ 3. Coach completes expectancy statement for the player (will include all responsibilities not scorecarded as stated above).

Second Meeting
(To be held within 7 days of first meeting.)

Date Completed

_____ 1. Player suggests additional areas for scorekeeping. (If agreed to by player and coach, these areas suggested by coach.)

_____ 2. Player requests support commitment from coach.

_____ 3. Player provides his expectancy statement.

Third Meeting
(To be completed within 7 days of second meeting.)

Date Completed

_____ 1. Player suggests minimum performance standards for these areas of measurement.

_____ 2. Player suggests pay-dirt levels and desired rewards.

_____ 3. Negotiation and agreement on all performance areas.

_____ 4. Review graph quadrants and agree on frequency of reporting.

_____ 5. Sign final agreements.

Fourth Meeting (and Contining Monthly Meetings)
(First fourth meeting to be completed within
thirty days of third meeting.)

1. Process Scorecard Review:
   a. Player presents scorecards in descending order.
   b. Coach provides appropriate feedback.
      i. If scorecard performance is in WOW zone – celebration.
      ii. If scorecard performance is in HOW zone – player suggests three plays he/she will execute during next 30-day period.
         1. Coach provides additional input on plays.
         2. Coach and player reach agreement on plays.

3. Plays are added to scorecard.
4. Plays are listed in descending order of importance.
5. Plays must be stated in the done sense, rather than the doing. (i.e. call 10 specific prospects, listed by name, is preferable to "doing a better job on my calling activity")

2. Projects Review
   a. Player presents list of projects accomplished during past 30-day period – We recommend this list be kept to three-five items.
   b. Coach provides suggestions for items for next 30 day list.
   c. Coach and player agree on items for list.
   d. Projects are listed in descending order of importance.
   e. List is provided to both coach and player.

   Last 30 Days Steps Completed
   1. _____
   2. _____
   3. _____

   Next 30 Days Steps Planned
   1. _____
   2. _____
   3. _____

We know that results are produced by behavior of all team members. We also recognize that coaching is based on taking the players where they don't believe they can get on their own. Coaches must be thinking of each player, not only in terms of the position they now play, but in terms of the positions they must be getting ready to play for the future success of the team and themselves. Since the heart of improved performance must be basedo n behavior change, this portion provides for that opportunity.

3. People Development Plan
   a. What behavior does the player need to stop doing?

   _____

   b. What behavior does the player need to accelerate doing?

   _____

   c. What behavior does the player need to start doing?

   _____

It is appropriate these behaviors listed will not change monthly, but rather be on the list until change has been completed, and the new behavior is part of the player.

All behavior changes must be written in duplicate for player and coach for reference between now and next coaching session.

The Game of Work, LLC
Field of Play
Monthly Plan

_____

Deadline Date

30-Days Priorities

1.

2.

3.

Directions:
    Be specific.
    State goals in "done" sense rather than "doing."

    1 copy to player
    1 copy to coach
    1 copy to contract file

The Game of Work, LLC
Field of Play
Coach's Expectations

1. Have a career orientation.

2. Be a conscientious counselor.

3. Support the performer.

4. Give 110 percent support, especially in front of members of The Game of Work team.

5. Be positive and specific.

6. Negatives come up to the coach. Positives go down to the players.

7. Write all unresolved questions at least weekly and send to me.

8. Expect growth through new tasks and assignments and techniques. Admit self-imposed limitations and attack past negative conditioning.

9. Be a product of the product. Personal goals and scorekeeping program current, up-to-date, and worthy to be demonstrated.

10. Expect and use "why" communication—if not provided, ask.

11. Trust coach's motives to have your best interests at heart.

A clearly outlined field of play results in certainty and consistency. And only after the field of play is established can realistic goals be set. You need to know where the field is before you can set the goals. In recreation we start with a clear definition of the boundaries, and we establish goals within those boundaries. In business, many times we start by establishing goals without first having the boundaries clearly in place. That's why it's often difficult to know if goals are realistic or not. The boundaries must precede the placement of goals in business as well as in sports.

To be an effective coach obviously requires more than creating a play book and a file cabinet full of field of play agreements. You must dedicate time to coaching.

The most effective way to do this is with a one-on-one uninterrupted coaching session with *each* player every month. *Every month.* If you are employing someone on a forty- hour week, or 173 hours a month, it isn't too much to ask that less than 1 percent of his time be earmarked for specific direction.

I know we give orders and instructions. We have staff meetings and team meetings and meetings to plan meetings. But I am talking here about coaching sessions, one-on-one, bare-knuckles, quality time taken with each individual player.

No coach would want to enter a critical game, part of a championship series, and have someone say, "Sorry, coach, you can't have any time-outs, no half-time with the players, no time between quarters." No coach would accept that, yet in business we seem perfectly willing to accept job descriptions with annual or semiannual review sessions.

Managers at The Game of Work and at the client companies who have adopted the game of work philosophy make sure that people are coached frequently and *regularly.* They do this with the cover page of the field of play agreement, which is a schedule agreed upon by player and coach as to the specific dates and times coaching sessions will take place. The field of play agreement is the most important document available in American business today. Why? Because it ensures that coaching and feedback will take place. It can be updated each month, or more often if performance (or lack thereof) warrants it. It is simple. It is straightforward. It is specific. Most of all, it is effective. The cover page of our field of play agreement looks like this:

The Game of Work, LLC

Field of Play Agreement

Between

Coach _____ Position _____
and _____ Position _____

1st Meeting Date_____ Coach _____ Player _____

2nd Meeting Date_____ Coach _____ Player _____

3rd Meeting Date_____ Coach _____ Player _____

**1st Monthly
Meeting** Date_____ Coach _____ Player _____

Feedback can never become too frequent, as long as it is honest and positive. Create a schedule so that your players know in advance when their hour arrives. If your span of control is too large for you to give this kind of quality coaching, spin off some of your people and build a second level of management. Get some assistant coaches. But do not hang onto a system that does not allow feedback from your people.

One of the biggest problems in business today is people are not being told what is expected of them. Every person has the right to personal freedoms and self-determination, but to get the job done—in sports as well as in business—somebody has to stand up and say, "This is what we are going to do, and this is how we are going to do it."

In the absence of a clearly defined field of play, uncertainty thrives and performance suffers. With a clearly defined field of play, players know the boundaries within which it is possible to win.

7

Winning

*Everybody is born with an equal chance to become
just as unequal as he or she possibly can.*

—Anonymous

Can you list the names of the four teams Pittsburgh beat in the Super Bowl? While you're working on that one, give me the three horses Seattle Slew beat to win the Triple Crown. And then after you get that, give me the five speed skaters that Eric Heiden beat to win his Olympic gold medals.

If you're having a tough time answering these questions, then just tell me who would hit the ground first if Saddam Hussein and Mohammar Kaddafi jumped off the Empire State Building at the same time. The answer is the same: Who cares? Don't let anybody tell you that winning isn't important.

There's a company in Salt Lake City that manufactures NFL insignia merchandise—part of a billion-dollar industry. The biggest customers are 25 to 29 year old fathers who didn't make it in football and are now hoping that through insignia osmosis the kid will do better.

Hundreds of companies throughout the country manufacture NFL merchandise. It's a billion dollar industry. Almost half of all NFL merchandise sold each year bears the logos of the Division Championship game participants. Why? Because everybody likes to do business with a winner.

Why do we use Olympic gold medalists and Super Bowl champions for all those shoe and drink commercials? Why don't we pick amateur athletes or semi-pro ball players? Wouldn't it be a lot cheaper? You know the answer. We pick the familiar because of the recognition value and the fact that everybody likes to do business with a winner.

Look at it this way. If you accidentally kill somebody with your car, who would you want to represent you in court? The top criminal attorney in the country with over a hundred wins under the belt, or some kid still in law school who thinks he or she can do a pretty good job but has never won a case in court? You would want to go with the winner, of course.

One of the premier high priests of winning in America was Vince Lombardi, former head coach of the Green Bay Packers. He said, "Winning isn't everything, it's the only thing."

The coach was criticized for that statement. Some said he placed too much emphasis on winning, that he should have put more emphasis on sportsmanship. Some of Lombardi's critics put together a new kind of baseball league for kids in a Texas community. It was like the Little League—the same ball, same bat, same number of innings, same playing field—everything was the same except that they didn't keep score. The idea was that there wouldn't be any losers because nobody would know who won.

Do you know how long it lasted? One and a half innings. The kids walked across the street to play sand-lot ball where they could keep score. Winning is important!

There's a lot being said today in America about fairness. Everything is supposed to be fair, and there are a lot of people who think that fair and equal are the same thing. Winners have a different philosophy that can be summed up in the following: "Everybody's born with the equal chance to become just as unequal as he or she possibly can."

A second thing Coach Lombardi said was, "The objective is to win fairly, squarely, by the rules, but to win." One of his great tackles, a guy by the name of Henry Jordan, had become a phenomenal salesman. Henry was asked one time, "Henry, why do you like to sell?" He said, "Because of the competition." He explained that every time a salesman meets a potential customer, a sale is made. Either the customer buys the product, or the salesman buys the customer's excuse.

A third thing Lombardi said is, "You don't win once in a while. You don't win occasionally. You don't win by accident. Winning is a habit, just like losing." Following are seven characteristics of winners.

1. *Winners are prepared.* Winners are ready to play. They don't show up for sales appointments without order forms. They don't show up without a game plan.

George Allen coached the Washington Redskins and took them to the Super Bowl. Allen paid a guy for a week to sit on the thirty-yard line in the Los Angeles Coliseum so he'd know what the angle of the sun would be during the entire ball game. Allen wanted to know which goal to defend when the coin was tossed. Winners are prepared.

How long does it take to reach the Super Bowl? The correct technical answer is twenty-four hours. That's right, twenty-four sixty-minute games—four preseason contests, sixteen regular season games, and four playoff contests—twenty-four hours of preparation are involved in preparing for each of those sixty-minute games? When you consider the time of the coaches, players, trainers—on and off the practice field—you wouldn't have any trouble counting up thousands of hours of preparation for each of those sixty-minute games.

In business, too often our dedication to constant activity eliminates the essential focus on preparation. If we are to be or to produce winners in our companies, we must take the time to prepare. We must take time to clearly define our Results to Resource Ratios for each of our key performers. We must take the time to give them the opportunity to construct a game plan, scout the competition, and build a strategy before we simply send them out to play.

2. *Winners expect to win.* Tiger Woods won three U.S. Amateur Championships before turning pro. Did he expect to win? You bet. In fact, the power of expectation was so strong, the man he beat in his third championship said, "I knew when I was only five holes up with nine to play, I didn't have a big enough lead."

Tiger Woods saw himself as a winner and made a bigger splash in the Amateur Golf Circuit than any in recent memory or maybe even of all time. That behavior continued on in his first major tournament victory. Less than three months later, he defeated an established veteran in sudden death. "I always expect to win, and I always expect the shot to go where I intend it go." It may be difficult to differentiate this self-assurance from unfounded cockiness, but the proof is in the performance. The winners always expect to win. Always.

Over a decade before, Broadway Joe Namath—upstart, young, and cocky—predicted that his team would win Super Bowl III. In the first two Super Bowls, the AFL champion had been beaten easily by the Green Bay Packers. And nobody expected the Baltimore Colts to stumble. But Joe Namath expected to win, and he delivered.

3. *Winners are specific and positive.* Losers tend to be general and negative. Negativism is the antithesis of a winning attitude. Negativism is the most destructive force that any of us come in contact with, because it robs us of those good feelings we should have about ourselves. Negativism is an evil force. Negativism is like a cancer of the mind.

I once had a young man working for me who was assigned the task of setting up sales calls, making appointments. He called in about 4:30 one afternoon, and I said, "How's it going, Richard?"

He said, "How do you get past these secretaries?"

"I don't understand," I said.

"None of them will let me see their bosses," he explained.

Any time I hear a negative generalization I immediately want to dig into it. I said, "Tell me how the day went."

"I made twenty calls," he said. "Fourteen of the bosses weren't even in."

I knew right off that 70 percent of the secretaries did not refuse to let him talk to their bosses. Their bosses weren't in.

"Tell me about the other six," I said.

"I got two appointments, and two people are going to call me back."

"The other two?"

"One had to leave in the middle of the conversation, and the other, well, her secretary . . ."

See what this salesman did? One of twenty calls went sour, so he made a negative generalization about the whole day's work. When you describe a negative situation, always be ultra-specific. Don't let the negative wandering generality rob you of a positive mental attitude.

Winners see their drinking glasses as half full, not half empty. Winners see the opportunity, losers see the problems. We have heard those comments before. If you have employees who are constantly looking at the empty half of the glass, you may want to focus on changing their performance *and* correcting their negative attitude.

4. *Winners accept personal responsibility for their actions.* Winners say "I," "me," and "our." Losers say "they," "them," "those guys," and "management." Losers use the language of noncommitment.

I was meeting with the manager of a company one time, and I asked, "Do you have any problems in this company?"

"Yes," he said, "we have two."

This is going to be easy, I thought. This guy has his problems all netted out.

"What is the first one?" I asked.

"Management doesn't care." As he spoke he extended his right arm straight to the ceiling and locked his elbow.

"What's the second one?" I asked.

"The employees don't care either." He extended his left arm toward the floor and again locked his elbow.

"May I ask you a question?" I asked.

He nodded.

"Which group do you fit into?"

He looked stunned. Finally, he said, "You know, I never thought of it like that before."

He had an acute case of loser's elbow. It's like tennis elbow, that ailment tennis players get when they serve too hard or don't hit the ball dead center.

Loser's elbow is most common in management and sales meetings. For instance, when the boss asks why the report isn't finished, somebody says, "Peggy didn't get it done." *Pop* goes the elbow. The boss asks why she didn't get it done. Somebody says, "The computer technician didn't get the network up." *Pop*, there it goes again. The computer technician gets blamed for most of the late reports in the world.

Another word popular with losers is *economy*. When the boss asks how sales were last month, the elbow goes pop when someone responds, "Well, you know how the economy is."

Inflation is another big word in the vocabularies of losers. Inflation is the sum total of all the increases in prices. Generally it affects your revenues as well as your expenses, the net difference being zero. That's all. Yet the decision-making politicians at the head of our government would like us to believe that inflation is the cause of our economic woes. They've got pains in their elbows, too.

Just as important in the language of noncommitment is *computer*. Ever hear of a shipment that didn't get out because of a computer? As if the computer is responsible for pulling the order, walking into the warehouse, and throwing a box on a truck. If computers were really responsible for half of what they get blamed for, companies would quit buying them.

Then there is the language of noncommitment related to places. Ever hear a receptionist say with the greatest tone of importance, "San Francisco's on the phone."

That would be something, a conference call with eight million people, all at once.

Or the guy who asks about the pay raise he was promised and is told that Chicago turned him down. And he didn't even know he was on the ballot.

The problem with loser's elbow is that your arm eventually locks into the losing position, making it tough for you to get through doorways when they open up. Somebody will say, "Hey, you did a super job on that project." And you will respond, "Well, not really, but wait until tomorrow." Winners accept personal responsibility, whether they are winning or losing.

The story of José and Juanita illustrates the acceptance of responsibility through the language of commitment.

It seems that José and Juanita were going to market early one morning and met at the crossroads.

"Good morning," said José.

"I'm not supposed to be talking to you," responded Juanita.

"And why not?" asked José, hurt by her blunt reply.

"José," she explained, "we are all alone here. There is no one else around. If I were to be friendly to you, you might attempt to steal a kiss."

"Juanita, how could I possibly do that?" he asked with a shocked look on his face but a slight gleam in his eye. "I am a merchant on the way to market. Underneath one arm I carry a live pig, and in that hand a washtub. Under the other arm I have a melon, and in that hand a live chicken."

"Even if I had a mind to commit such a bold act," he continued, "I could not do so for fear of losing my entire inventory."

"No, José," responded Juanita, without hesitation. "You could place the pig on the ground and put the washtub over him. Then you could put the melon on top to hold it in place. And then I could hold the chicken."

Juanita was a winner and was willing to take responsibility for her own actions. She did not use the language of noncommitment.

Resolve today to eliminate loser's elbow from your organization. When you are in a sales meeting or a one-on-one conversation and someone starts speaking in the language of noncommitment—"I'm not responsible," "It's somebody else's job"—simply extend your elbow out in any direction, snapping it quickly, and explain the principle of loser's elbow. Then they will begin to understand this all-important principle of winning in the game of work. We, as coaches, have the responsibility to establish the emotional and attitudinal climate of our team, our company, our business—and there should be no place for loser's elbow, the language of noncommitment.

5. *Winners don't seek to change the rules.* They seek only to understand them well enough to win.

At the 1996 Olympic Games in Atlanta, the United States women's gymnastics team was marching toward the gold medal when Kerri Strug, the team's last performer in the last event, severely sprained her ankle. Talk about bad timing. Here they are, on the verge of collecting America's first ever women's team gymnastics gold medal, needing just one more vault to hold off the Russians and lock it up, and suddenly the athlete who's supposed to perform that vault is having a hard time standing up.

It was at this point of the competition, with an estimated billion people watching around the world, that Bela Karolyi, Strug's coach, marched over to the Russian coach and said, "OK, our girl's hurt. We'll count what she did yesterday, when both her ankles were healthy. Got to keep this thing fair."

You don't remember that? Of course you don't. That's not the way winners behave. Instead, Karolyi shouted out to his athlete, "Come on Kerri, you can do it. This is what you've trained for."

Kerri got up and limped back to the head of the runway. She had just seventy-five seconds to complete her vault. After another glance at her coach she started running. She vaulted high into the air, executed a twisting one and a half somersault, and landed solidly on both feet. She even managed a kind of "take that!" smile in the direction of the judge before she lifted her aching ankle off the mat once she'd "stuck" her landing. Kerri Strug knew that the rules don't change, that it's your performance that you're judged on.

Think about all the people who are trying to change the rules today. They are trying so hard to make things fair and equal that they never get into the real game where they can win.

We will always have leaders and followers, winners and losers, people who add to and people who take away. A lot of things need changing, but winners don't try to change the rules in the middle of the game; they seek only to understand them well enough to win.

Jay Van Andel, one of the founding partners of the Amway Corporation, delivered during his service as chairman of the board of the United States Chamber of Commerce, a speech containing a truly great quotation about a lesson this country needs to learn: "We are not going to help the caboose catch up to the engine by stopping the train." Certainly we need to seek change and improvement, but too many people are trying to change the rules for an easy shortcut or a free lunch so they can receive the benefits of winning without having to play the game.

6. *Winners pay the price—willingly, because they know it's a bargain.*

How many times have you heard this one?

"If you want to be a winner, you've got to pay the price?" And they always say it as if they had just had a dill pickle.

"Pay the price, it's going to hurt."

"No pain, no gain."

"Take another ten laps. Don't stop when the blisters pop."

Losers pay a price too, but winners pay it *willingly*.

Eric Heiden is a real winner. He won five gold medals at Lake Placid for the best individual performance ever in the Winter Olympic Games. He is from Wisconsin. His schedule included starting on the university soccer team and then running the 289 steps up the ski-jump hill. Plus, he skated in those subzero winters wearing that thin racing suit.

But he didn't train outside all the time. He has a training room equipped with a stainless steel platform about seven feet wide with a four-inch lip around the edge. In training for the Olympics he got on the platform and exercised four hours at a time, day after day, week after week, year after year. They showed it on television, and what kind of expression do you think was on Eric's face.

There was no agony, pain, or disappointment. Just a smile, the expression of a winner. And behind the camera, in full view, Eric could see a picture of the gold medals he was going to win. Winners pay the price willingly because they know it's a bargain. And when you concentrate on the end result, the obstacles melt away in the intensity of the preparation.

Winners are more willing to pay the price as the coach becomes more skilled at painting vivid pictures of the end results or benefits. Putting the *why* into our communication brings about incredible performances from the players.

7. *Winners set goals.* Winning and goal-setting are synonymous. You can't win unless you know what victory represents. There are a lot of losers who work just as hard as the people who win, but they never figure out when to stop and celebrate. But, most of all, winners are goal-setters.

Tiger Woods came on the golf scene in the mid '90's like a hurricane unseen in 30 years. Winner of three U.S. Amateur Championships, he was a "winner" from his first tee shot. Did he just fall there? No, of course not. Almost since birth, the goals had been set. Set for him at first, and then accepted by, embraced by and internalized by Tiger himself. He was a star on the Mike Douglas Show at 3, hitting shots at 11 months, waking up every morning with the press clippings of Jack Nicklaus, and the other greats he would first emulate and then eclipse surrounding him. Few before him and none since had won the first major they played as a professional. How did he do it? "Huge goals. He has huge goals, and only when you have huge goals can you accomplish great things," was the quote from one of those who found themselves in that historic 1997 Masters competing for second place. Could he win the Grand Slam, Masters, U.S. Open, British Open, and PGA championship in a single season? His response, "on paper it is possible!" Who among us is foolish enough to believe it is not also possible in his heart. Winners are Goal Setters, and more importantly Goal Getters.

Winners are goal setters, and the rise or fall of every organization is based on the ability of individuals in those organizations to set and achieve goals. Setting a clear goal will give you more motivation than someone holding a gun to your head or a thousand dollar bill in front of your nose.

Remember Dorothy Hamill? She won a gold medal and the world figure-skating championships at age seventeen. Then she landed a lucrative advertising contract with Clairol.

Dorothy set her goal when she was six years old. She got up at five in the morning and practiced for two hours before school, where she maintained a B+ average. After school she practiced for two more hours, day after day, week after week, year after year, for eleven years until she reached her goal.

Goal-setting is the strongest force in the world for human motivation.

But you don't have to be an Olympic athlete or a professional football player to make goals work. You don't have to start as a kid, either.

In his autobiography, Harland Sanders, founder of Kentucky Fried Chicken, tells about the Great Depression. He said he thoughtfully planned a scheme for kidnapping and holding for ransom the child of a wealthy neighbor to buy food. He was flat broke four times. He was cooking chicken in his wife's restaurant because he couldn't make it in the motel business.

The Colonel cooked his first piece of Kentucky Fried Chicken at 3900 South State Street in Salt Lake City when he was sixty-five years old. Then he left for a few weeks. When he came back the place had gone wild. Everybody wanted that Kentucky Fried Chicken.

At seventy-two he sold out to Johnny Y. Brown, ex-football player and former governor of Kentucky. The Colonel received $2 million plus $250,000 a year in personal appearance contracts.

Harland Sanders has the most recognized face in the world, next to Mickey Mouse. At age eighty-eight he was asked if he had any more goals. "Yup," he said. "I've got three of them. Number one, I'd like to live twelve more years and become a centenarian. Second, at 100 I would like to take two years off, because I haven't had a vacation since I cooked that first piece of chicken, and I'm getting tired. Third, after I get off my vacation at 102, I'd like to come back with a new idea and make another major impact on American life." Leukemia took him at age 90, so he never reached those last goals. Still, goal setting is the strongest force in the world for human motivation.

A little over three percent of the people in the United States are considered financially independent. Do you have any idea what minimum net worth is required to be included in that select category? A million dollars, perhaps. Actually a good guess.

According to the book, "The Millionaire Next Door," there are approximately 3.5 percent of the households in the United States with a net worth in excess of $1,000,000. That net worth is accompanied by an average annual income just over $135,000 per year.

Ten percent of the households have a net worth between $350,000 and $1,000,000. They earn between $80,000 and $120,000 per year. These people are deemed by the reporters to be financially comfortable.

Sixty percent of the people in the United States barely make a living. Their net worth is tied up primarily in the homes they live in, and it is mostly offset with charge card balances.

Twenty-seven percent of the people need some form of outside support just to survive. It fluctuates depending on who is in the White House.

What do you think distinguishes the top two groups from the bottom two, other than the fact that the top two are where everyone wants to be? The top two groups are goal oriented, while those in the bottom group have few goals, if any. Still, the 3 percent group, on the average, outperforms the ten percent group fifty to one. The average net worth of the 3 percent group is many times greater than the average net worth of the ten percent group. Yet there are no demographic differences between the two groups—no significant differences in age, race, religion, education, sex, and parental wealth. (See David C. McClelland, *The Achieving Society* [New York: Free Press, 1967].)

The big difference is that the people in the three percent group have prepared written goals with specific plans for reaching those goals. Not very many people are willing to do that.

Why don't people like to set goals? Why don't people like to write them down? Some people don't like to measure performance—fear of failure, perhaps. Some people are lazy. But look at what they are passing up. Rich people live longer and better and seem to be more happy. And, contrary to all the publicity, the people in this group have fewer divorces.

Franklin D. Roosevelt constructed his plan for the Presidency of the United States twenty years before he was elected. The world's greatest and most beautiful buildings, bridges, and airplanes are first created, in elaborate detail, on the drawing board before the first brick or piece of metal is set in place.

Writing goals allows us to transfer our dreams into a specific plan that can be handed to others to work on. Written goals are not opinions or whims or wishes. Writing goals is the key step that turns dreams into reality. It makes the difference between losing and winning.

We must be the architect of our own lives. Who do you go to when you are preparing to build your dream house? That's correct, the architect. And why? Why would any of us spend the six to eight percent of the total value of the house on the architect? In a $1,000,000 home that extra $60,000 or $80,000 could make a substantial difference in amenities. Why then do we commit that portion of the budget to this discipline? Because the architect takes the hazy ideas in our minds, and reduces them to written plans—so that others can help in doing the work. Does it not make perfect sense that if this skill is important in the creation of a home, that we need the same skill in the way we live the remainder of our lives?

8

Attitudes of Winners

If you are going to be a successful duck hunter,
you must go where the ducks are.

—Paul "Bear" Bryant

In 1978, when I was just beginning to see the many parallels between sports and business, I decided to interview some real winners. I got on the phone and called Alabama. I wanted to talk to Paul "Bear" Bryant, who has since passed away but was then head football coach at the University of Alabama.

I just dialed the area code and asked for "The Bear." Immediately the operator put me through to this man who had become a legend in his own time. In 1982 the Alabama legislature met to pass an exception to its mandatory age seventy retirement law. The Addendum stated that the Bear could work for the state of Alabama as long as he pleased. That's how much they thought of that man in Alabama.

When I got him on the phone I asked him if he was a winner. He growled, "I won 307 football games. I won 88.7 percent of all the ball games I ever coached."

I got the message. He was specific. I thanked him for his time and hung up the phone.

Then I called the head football coach at a local state university, a major university with national recognition in many areas, thinking he too would know about winning. I asked him if he was a winner.

He said, "Chuck, you've got to understand something."

Right away I knew I was in trouble.

"You've got to understand," he said, "that I've got the seventh smallest budget in the conference. If I finish higher than seventh, I'm not doing bad."

I thought maybe he didn't hear me, so I repeated the question: "Coach, are you a winner?"

"Chuck," he said, "you've got to understand that they don't support football in this town the way they do down the highway (at the conference champion school)."

I thought I'd give him one more shot. I said, "Coach, are you a winner?"

He said, "Do you know how hard it is to get those kids from Southern California to come up here and play football?"

My conversation with the coach reminded me of a retail clothing store I did some work with. I asked the president of the company what he would most like us to do for him.

"I'd like to have you stop the weather reports," he said.

I didn't know what he was talking about and asked him to explain. He did.

"I've got these eight retail stores out there," he said, "and every time I call up and ask how sales are, they give me the weather report. If I ask if everybody showed up for work, they say it's snowing and the people couldn't get in. Or the customers had to stay home because it's raining. Just stop the weather reports!"

What this manager really wanted was for me to get his employees looking at the scorecards and goals instead of making excuses for bad performance. He wanted specifics, not generalities. Winners are specific.

Winners Play the Odds

One time a reporter was interviewing Willie Sutton, the famous bank robber. The reporter was trying to gain insights into the criminal mind in an effort to better understand criminal behavior.

"Willie, why do you rob banks?" asked the reporter in all sincerity.

"Because that's where the money is," responded Willie.

Like Willie, winners understand probabilities. They go where the money is. They understand the Pareto Principle. Pareto, history tells us, was an Italian sociologist who studied tax rolls and tax rates and concluded that 20 percent of the property owners paid 80 percent of the property taxes. I don't know what that discovery did for Mr. Pareto, but I know it is a hot subject in business circles. You and I know it as the 80-20 Principle.

I once had the opportunity to work with a communications firm that was leading in its market—they had it made. I remember one of their salesmen, a seven-year veteran, a man well past the middle of his life. He was the kind of person who's hard to motivate because he already has most of the material things he wants in life. He was the number-four producer in the sales network, one of those solid individuals you just build the company around. He was the good old boy.

As we began to meet, he was always saying that he was too busy for my goal setting gimmicks. He had a lot of work to do, things that had to be attended to, and people to call on—hustle, hustle, hustle. My goal setting wouldn't work for him because I didn't understand his business and I didn't understand the market.

He was a hustler, a hard worker. He had a plan: he would go out and work hard, hope he sold a lot, try to develop new accounts, get that extra business, and make the goals. He knew he was really good. The commission checks just rolled in. He was typical—too typical.

I introduced him to the 80-20 Principle—that 20 percent of his accounts produced 80 percent of his business.

"Chuck," he responded, "you don't understand this business at all."

As we continued our debate, I asked him to consider the investment in my services his company had already made, and I asked him to try it my way, just once. I asked him to take his previous year's sales records and go back and calculate how much of his business came from each customer and to rank them according to dollars spent with him.

He reluctantly agreed to follow my suggestion and returned just a week later with a satisfied look on his face, as if he had proven something to somebody.

"You said that 20 percent of my accounts would be 80 percent of my volume," he said.

"That's true," I responded.

"You were wrong," he said. But along with that look of satisfied defiance, I noticed a little hint that he may have learned something as well.

"How far off was I?" I asked.

"The top 19 accounts, out of a total of 104, accounted for 83 percent of my business," he said, as he and the rest of the people in the room began to laugh.

"I want you to know too," he continued, "that another 6 of my accounts produced the next 13 percent of my volume, and that 25 of my 104 accounts produced 96 percent of all the dollar volume I did last year."

"How do you feel?" I said.

"Wonderfully embarrassed."

"What are you going to do now?"

"I'm going to take the bottom 40 accounts," he said, "and lay them on the sales manager's desk with a note that I don't deserve to work with them."

He did that, and the sales manager was shocked and immediately created a draft pool to redistribute accounts to new sales people.

The salesman said he was going to major on the majors. He laid out a schedule over the next 90 days to meet with each of his accounts in descending order from the largest to the smallest. The time that would have been spent on the 40 accounts he didn't have anymore, he used to identify and penetrate into new business that had the potential to compete in size with his best clients.

Four months later he told me he had just received his largest commission check since coming to work for the company. He had paid off a couple of second mortgages on his different investment properties, and he and his wife were enjoying a lifestyle unparalleled in their history. An understanding of the 80-20 Principle had enabled him to major on the majors, thanks to a simple scorekeeping technique.

Incidentally, he came into my program with a goal to increase sales by 13 percent. Ninety days later he revised it to 47 percent, then exceeded that and achieved a 55 percent increase in sales the first 12 months after starting a tracking system. The tracking system enabled him to motivate himself without outside pressure, to realize more of his own untapped potential.

The 80-20 Principle can be graphically illustrated for any business or sales person as shown on the chart on the following page.

Majoring on the majors can produce these same results for your team. The marketplace defines how the team is doing. Major on making the strong stronger.

In industrial sales accounts there is a fairly safe, yet aggressive application of the 80-20 Principle that can result in dramatic results when the customer base is reasonably constant.

First, take the 20 percent of your accounts that account for 80 percent of your business and establish a goal for a 25 percent increase in that group of accounts. If accomplished, this increase can replace all the business obtained from the other 80 percent of the accounts. Any business at all from the other 80 percent will be increased business. This is the first step.

The second step is to take the next 40 percent of your accounts that traditionally accounted for about 16 percent of your business and set a goal to double the business from this group of accounts. This is a reasonable, logical plan, giving you the opportunity to build a 32 percent increase into your sales and still generate excess accounts that are available for redistribution to young, aggressive new sales people.

I have had a lot of success, and fun, teaching companies how to manage the pool of leftover accounts. We have set up a system similar to the NFL draft, where the lowest producing salesperson gets first draft pick from the pool, the next to the lowest salesperson

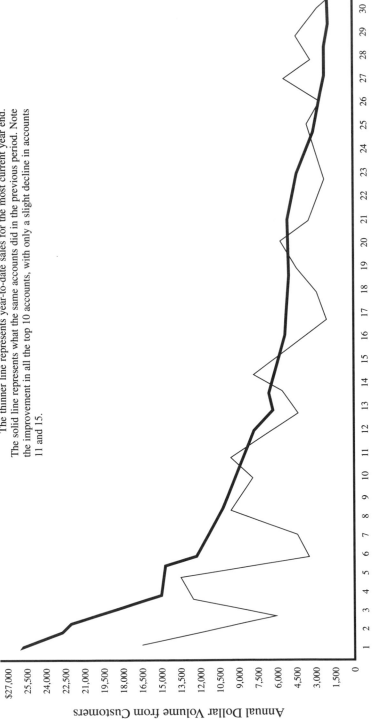

Client Expenditures
Before and After Application of 80-20 Principle

The thinner line represents year-to-date sales for the most current year end. The solid line represents what the same accounts did in the previous period. Note the improvement in all the top 10 accounts, with only a slight decline in accounts 11 and 15.

Annual Dollar Volume from Customers

$27,000
25,500
24,000
22,500
21,000
19,500
18,000
16,500
15,000
13,500
12,000
10,500
9,000
7,500
6,000
4,500
3,000
1,500
0

1 2 3 4 5 6 7 8 9 10 11 12 13 14 15 16 17 18 19 20 21 22 23 24 25 26 27 28 29 30 31

getting the second pick, and so on. At the end of the draft, the salespeople are given a short period for trading. Then, in 30 days, each salesperson is expected to turn in to the sales manager a written plan of attack for each of the new accounts. At the end of this process any leftover accounts are turned over to the inside order desk to become house accounts or to be part of a telemarketing program.

Frequently it's necessary to differentiate between types of productivity analyzed. Inventory, for example, can be subdivided into different items or groups of items with varying turnover rates. Again the 80-20 Principle can be applied. Often, 20 percent of the items in inventory account for 80 percent of the sales volume.

Several years ago I helped a paint distributor get his inventory under control. I asked him how he tracked individual products. He said he didn't need to because he had established a company goal to have everything in stock 100 percent of the time, a goal so often emphasized that it simply didn't need to be tracked.

Finally, after much discussion, he agreed to spend $10 worth of a clerk's time to measure the company's actual ability to have on hand the desired product 100 percent of the time. We discovered during the first week, in the middle of the prime selling season, that 17 percent of the orders couldn't be shipped because of insufficient inventory. The president was flabbergasted.

"We can't have this," he said. "It must have been an unusual week."

We agreed to continue the tracking, and in the second week 16 percent of the orders couldn't be shipped because of the insufficient inventory. The president was beginning to listen. He agreed to continue the tracking until we achieved the desired results.

Within two and a half months we had the number of unfillable orders down to six percent. But we weren't satisfied. The inventory was too large. And there was some question about the value of our measurements.

We acknowledged the 80-20 Principle and agreed that there needed to be differentiation between different inventory items, with more emphasis where the greater problems existed. We divided the inventory into three groups. Exactly 20 percent of the items fell into group A, which comprised 78 percent of total sales. Management resolved to never be out of stock on these items. We tracked them separately from the other two groups.

Group B consisted of 40 percent of the items responsible for 17 percent of sales. We agreed that these were necessary items to stock, but not imperative for the success of the organization. Frequently these items were the same product as in group A, but in different-sized containers. Sometimes they were paints where the color was just a shade off the group A color. Often substitutions could be made if these items were out of stock. We determined that with group B items the company could maintain a higher risk of running out.

Group C, the bottom 40 percent of the inventory, accounted for less than five percent of total sales. The president was amazed that he had so much money tied up in such a small part of his business. It was obvious that the company could accept a much higher out-of-stock risk with items that made up such a small part of the business. We concluded that with many of the items it would be better to air freight them in than tie up so much capital in inventory.

We established criteria for each inventory level, measured by weeks on hand. In group A we decided that in the peak season we would attempt to carry an eight-week supply. In group B we decided to carry a two-week supply, maintaining a six-week average for all inventory. For group C we maintained no safety level, just one item on the shelf to be reordered when it was sold.

We began to beef up orders for group A items to get to the eight-week level, and we reduced orders for group B and group C items. As we finished the busy season, we had reduced the inventory from $290,000 to $165,000 and banked $115,000 of former operating capital, while maintaining a customer order satisfied record of 93 percent. By keeping score you can have your cake and eat it too.

In business we often hear—and my father, the grocer, has repeated it many times—that we cannot afford to ignore any customer. Every one is important. Although this is true, applications of the 80-20 Principle occur so often and with such force that it cannot be ignored.

If you are going to hunt ducks, you must go where the ducks are. And if you are going to kill giants, you must spend your time in the beanstalks, not in the pea vines. After consulting in detail with hundreds of businesses, I don't hesitate to say that there are applications of the 80-20 Principle in every business.

Losers refuse to face up to such facts. That is why they lose. But winners face up to what is really happening—they even keep track of it. That winning attitude gives them the knowledge they need to win.

9

Results to Resources Ratio

*If winning isn't important, why do we spend
all that money on scoreboards?*

—Chuck Coonradt

In business, one of the most effective measurement devices is return on investment. It may be expressed in several ways: return on assets, return on equity, return on net capital invested, or return on net assets. Return on investment measures the amount of profitability one can generate with certain assets, be they inventory, people, cash, real estate, or equipment. We do very well in using this measurement on an overall company level. We do very well in using this measurement on an overall company level. We look at it annually—it's always in the annual report. And we may even evaluate it quarterly, but seldom more frequently than that.

There is a parallel in recreation and sports. We can use the term Results to Resource Ratio, or the RRR. In athletics, baseball for example, there are several Results to Resource Ratios. Batting championships are decided on the batting average, the relationship between the number of at bats (resource) and then number of hits (results). The RRR for a league leader will be in the high .300s, perhaps over .375. The greatest batter in history by this measurement was Ted Williams, who batted .406 for an entire season. Batting average is an RRR.

In football we have an RRR for practically every member of

to permit the play to develop, be it a pass blocking assignment or a running block. The number of opportunities or the number of plays in which a lineman blocks versus the number of times he holds the block for the required number of seconds reflect that RRR.

As we move into what are called the skill positions, those which come in contact with the ball, we have an even larger number of Results to Resource Ratios. Receiver performance is measured in total receptions, receptions per game, yards per reception or game, number of games over a hundred yards, and total yardage for the season. In fact, in all sports computers constantly measure results to resources for all of the players and generate beautiful computer graphics for explaining those numbers to the fans via television.

In golf, the money becomes the most important measurement. Everybody knows how much the top golfers earn. But along with that we have expanded RRRs, including average strokes per round. We have a driving percentage, which is the number of drives placed in the fairway; the approach percentage, which is the number of approaches effectively delivered to the green from within 200 yards; and a putting percentage, or putts per round. These RRRs are measured in one-hundredths of strokes, even though the smallest increment of measurement in golf is one stroke. The experts recognize that if you put together all of the measured elements of the game consistently, with the right timing, you will come away with a victory.

The Results to Resource Ratio is also essential in effectively managing a business. It's the key relationship between the stockholders and the management team. We must ask ourselves two questions: Why is it necessary? And why has it not been expanded further into management circles?

There are two reasons. One, we have never understood the obvious importance of the RRR in business. Two, we have never defined the fundamental way in which it is put together. Managers are inhibited or intimidated by this process. Let's set forth the method for constructing an RRR.

Divide a sheet of paper with one vertical line as in the diagram below. At the top of one side write "Resources." At the top of the other write "Results." For this example, let's use a controller in a medium-size organization who has a staff responsible for all the fundamental management accounting reports, payroll, accounts payable, accounts receivable, and so on. It might be easier to look at a mail sorter, salesperson, or lathe operator—but if we can do it for a controller, we can do it for anybody.

Now we may ask ourselves initially what her resources are. Some of the words come easily: time, subordinates, know-how, equipment, calculators, electronic typewriters, word processors. She also has a resource of space occupied by administrative people, space that cannot be assigned to sales or manufacturing or the productivity side of the business.

Results to Resource Ratio

Resources	Results
Time:	
Hours	
Minutes	

We must ask ourselves one major question: How do I measure the ingredients? When I write down "time," how do I measure it?

The easiest way, of course, is in hours and minutes. And so below "time" I write down the amount of time this person has available to her—forty or forty-eight hours a week. As a footnote, we may take the amount of time that she feels productive, the time she really feels she has to manage. (If you were measuring the time resources of an entrepreneur, you may pick the number of hours she spends away from her family.)

Now we go to subordinates' time. Again, it is measured in at least two ways. One is hours at work. You may look at an employee and write down his total departmental person-hours based on a forty-hour week, 4.3 weeks in a month, or 172 hours times the number of people on the staff. With a five-person department, he would have in excess of eight hundred hours plus the controller's hours on a monthly basis. A second way to measure the labor resource is in dollars of labor cost. We're beginning to define our resource.

Now, the machine time. We may look at that in dollars or in hours. We might look at the entire budget, including person-hours, space, and time in terms of an overall dollar cost for the business or any particular department.

As the manager begins to define resources, something becomes very apparent: resources in most organizations are easier to define than results. Selecting the right results is the essence of effective management by measurement.

Resources	Results
Time—800 person-hours	
Space—1,500 square feet	
Equipment—$7,000 a month	

Let's take the same approach on the right side of the chart. What results are we looking for from the controller? If you look at her job description, or the understanding she obtained in Accounting 101 in college, you will find words like: provide management with *timely, accurate, and complete* financial information to *profitably* conduct the affairs of the business organization.

Now, let's list each of the desired results: timely, accurate, and complete reporting, Behind each of these results we write a method of measuring them. If we are looking for accuracy, we might look at a percentage error factor. If we are looking for timeliness, we might look at a variance between when reports were promised and when they were delivered. If we're looking for completeness, we can use either of the two previous statements.

Resources   Results

> Timely — Difference between regular pro-
> ject promise dates and delivery
> dates.
> Accurate — 1. Errors per number of items
> prepared.
> 2. Number of times a report
> must be prepared to be accurate.
> Profitable — 1. Net profit for entire company.
> 2. Net or gross profit generated
> by an individual department.

Now we want to identify the most expensive resource and the most valuable result and see if they can be combined. For example, we might look at this controller and her staff and conclude that the human element is, in fact, the most expensive resource we have. So let's underline that on the left-hand side of our chart. Next we'll go to the result side and ask ourselves the same question. What is our most valuable result? We might look, even though the controller is not in total control, at profit as the most important result we're looking for. We can then construct a preliminary ratio of net profit dollars per total department hours. *Net profit dollars per total department hours*—that's our Results to Resources Ratio.

Resources	Results
People	Timely
Space	Accurate
Equipment	Profitable

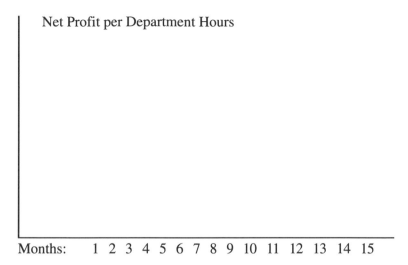

Net Profit per Department Hours

Months: 1 2 3 4 5 6 7 8 9 10 11 12 13 14 15

When you come up with a new RRR that becomes a measurement of someone's productivity or output, these questions invariably pop up: What does it mean? Even if we looked at it and found out what it said, what would it really mean? Is it worthwhile to keep track of it? We've never done this before. What are the measurements? Where do they go? Well, we recognize as managers that a number-one priority is to minimize the uncertainty on our team.

So, having constructed a new look, we must first expect to encounter some resistance. If we are able to do our research in such a fashion that we can look at historical data and assemble it in new terms before we necessarily expose our players to the information, we then have a tremendous opportunity to tell them what the new measurement means and reduce their fear and apprehension quickly.

For example, one of my clients recently went back and identified his net income per employee-hour for the last five years. He found change in the ratio from year to year of the following magnitude:

	Year	1	2	3	4	5
Profit increases						
Wage increases		31%	27%	15%	11%	4%
Net gain in productivity per dollar paid		9%	11%	14%	17%	18%
		22%	18%	1%	(6%)	(14%)

Profit: ——————

Wages: --------------

Productivity: ▬▬▬▬

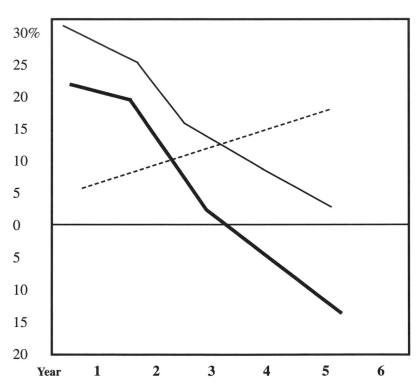

With this historical perspective, the chairman of the board committed the human resources manager to provide a plan for subsequent staffing, not based on opinion, observation, or judgment, but on a measurement of a Results to Resource Ratio.

The important concept here is to get the RRR to reflect accurately the philosophies and intent of the organization. For example, we might conclude that in a typical growing, developing organization, after the initial addition of computers and personnel to the accounting department, the relationship between total accounting department expenses and sales would begin to decline. Procedures would become routine as the company begins to grow. After all, it takes only a marginally greater amount of time to process twice the number of invoices. The input times are not doubled for orders that are twice as big. We need only one vice president controller. We will tend to fill in with lower wage scale people. Our average hourly rate should come down with the passing of time. And so I think we could make a case for the fact that the RRR we call sales per administrative person-hour might be expected to rise over time.

I love to bet that if you track any company over a ten year period, you will find that without measurement by management those costs have in fact not decreased but increased, and that the sales per administrative hour have gone down over time in spite of inflationary pressure to increase prices. We are, in most instances, doing less work with more people today than we were ten years ago.

If the computer is justifiable—reducing turn-around time and making a contribution to the organization over the cost of that computer—there should be real savings when you add the cost of the new resource to the resource side of our chart.

Before you accuse me of unrelenting conservativism, let me point out that it is not my purpose to impose a direction on your business. If you wish to increase your administrative costs as a percentage of sales, that's your business and your right. My point is that you need to know what is happening, to know if you are winning or losing. Management must provide workers or supervisors with a realistic and clearly defined expectation so that they have a chance of knowing whether they are winning or losing. The purpose of the RRR is to do that very thing.

Included in the concept of a RRR is the *per.* Sales *per* manhour. Yards *per* game. Yards *per* carry. The *per* triggers the relationship between results and resources.

Every professional has *pers.* Every member of my management team has them. Every member of yours will want to develop them.

A word of caution: The concept of measurement is sometimes regarded as punitive and must therefore be approached carefully and sold to the players as a benefit.

When salespeople are in trouble, they have to call home more often. When a business has financial problems, we may call in the auditors, who count clearly and frequently until we fix the problem. Once it is fixed, almost denying the power of measurement and frequent feedback, the auditors leave and take the measurement system with them, and we are again left on our own with less feedback than we had when we were in the problem mode, somehow feeling that we should continue to muddle through until business goes bad again, knowing that the auditors will return.

How do you gain a commitment to measurability? How do you reach inside and turn that switch on? We'll discuss that more in the chapter on motivation, but let me suggest that there are some levels of involvement that can be developed.

I mentioned earlier the advantage of a historical perspective. Take, for example, an accountant's receivables. It is easy to go back and create a thirty-six-month timeline showing the pattern of days of sales outstanding, as on the following page

If the information is generated and processed by the players, you teach the players the formula. As they go back over the past

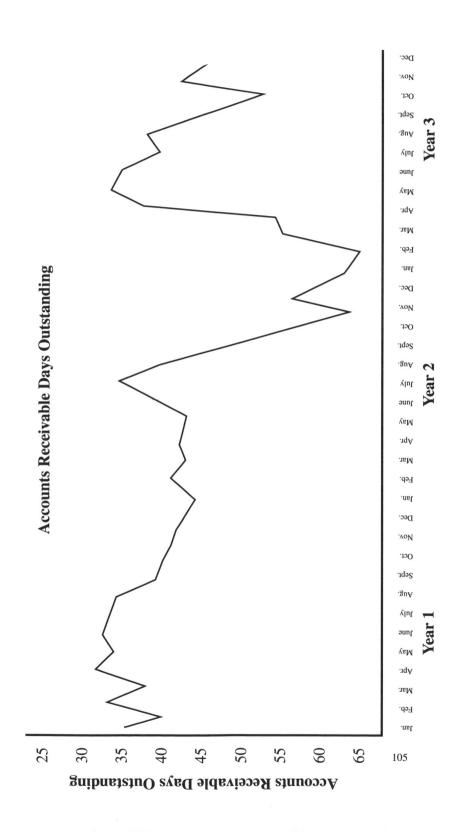

Accounts Receivable Days Outstanding

eighteen months or so and generate their own calculations and their own graphs, the impression on them will be substantial, much better than if the graph is presented to them by someone else. It will be better to have them go dig out the information to have someone else graph it. If you want to understand something, do it yourself—touch it, chart it, study it. The self-administration of a management measurement program is the very best way to generate commitment to the process.

An alternative form, if you have a highly resistant subordinate or player, or if you're attempting to influence a peer level where the authority may be less than clearly defined, is to benefit by going back and constructing a graph and sharing that information with the players who are responsible for that area of performance. It will give them a broader concept of the point you wish to make in training or challenging.

If people can be sold on keeping score, out of curiosity or in an effort to do something fun with their job, you have succeeded. *If you can, through motivational communication, provide them with the* why *in your thinking and share with them the importance of their participation, you will have a commitment that will last as long as you continue to reinforce it.* The RRRs can be sold and merchandised.

An important part of the effective installation of a management measurement system is that the leadership must lead the way by example. So, before imposing the idea on your subordinates or simply handing a copy of this book to someone and wishing them well, look around your own field of play and determine what your RRRs are. Make several lists, several pages. Look for various combinations. Look for the resource that is most expensive and the result that is most desirable. Some examples are: number of smiles per day, number of transactions per employee labor hour, days of sales of inventory on hand, working days of billings outstanding in accounts receivable, average billing days deposited per month in the cash deposits area, number of phone calls made between successful appointments, number of presentations between sales. The list goes on and on. Be tough on yourself and you will be more effective with your people. Get behind the idea. Get involved in it and get interested in it, and you will find that you can be the coach, the leader, and the team captain we all want so much on our team.

You may not, on your first attempt, come up with a perfect measurement, but if you will begin, if you will have the courage to try it and watch closely your own results, you will be more capable of producing results in others.

10

Picking Winners

Freedom is greatest when the boundaries are clearly defined.

—Chuck Coonradt

Every year before the NFL draft begins, the teams have a lot of data to study, years of college statistics and scouting reports that may go as far back as high school. They have numerous personal observations to back up the numerical data.

In business, most of us do not have that kind of information to help us pick winners for our team. Its easy to pay Shaquille O'Neal millions of dollars after he has proven himself, but its a lot tougher to snatch an 18-year-old high school graduate coming out early and give him a lot of money in the expectation that a few years down the road he'll become a star performer. By contrast in business, we must interview and hire people we know little about, but whom we have the responsibility to discover, nurture, and turn to value the untapped potential. And in many cases, immediately.

How do you do it? Simple, although not easy! Look for the numbers, not the number of schools they attended. Look for results, the candidates track records in similar positions. And most importantly, search for their willingness to be accountable and scorable in the new position.

In sports they always check the numbers. When a baseball club trades pitchers for hitters, or fielders for coaches, they don't worry about the personality or who the person went to high school with. They care about performance, statistics. The key to picking winners is to get as close to the attributes we listed in the chapter on winning as possible. And when you can't get numbers, you look for heart. And how do you do that?

First, winners believe in themselves and see a relationship between past accomplishments and the future assignment. They can't have this if the future assignment isn't clearly spelled out. Good feelings about past success must be transferred to the new assignment.

Sometimes a wise manager may recognize qualities in recruits beyond what the new employees can see in themselves. The coach of a Super Bowl team once said, "Coaching is merely taking them someplace they don't think they can go on their own."

As a general rule, your most likely winner is the person who can find a direct relationship between past successes and the new assignment. By the time some successful college basketball players reach the NCAA Final Four, they have lost only a dozen games in their careers, since grade school. You wouldn't hire a talented offensive lineman to play quarterback. You want someone who has had success that can be associated with the new assignment.

Second, winners have commitment to the team's direction. They see a direct relationship between the company's goals and their own individual goals. In sports, these are the players who can see a relationship between the hours and hours of practice and the few moments of glory and recognize that as a bargain.

Third, you're looking for coachability. For every recognized winner there is a coach in the background. Winners recognize that good coaches have knowledge and information beyond their own capabilities, and they are willing to assimilate this through the coach. They are open to the leadership of others. The great ones have mentors.

On the locker room wall at Michigan State University there used to be a sign that said, "The difference between good and great is a little extra effort." The word *little* was emphasized.

The rewards in sports usually don't accurately represent the "little" differences between winners and those who finish second. Each year on the PGA Golf Tour the winners are ranked by total earnings. In 1996 Tom Lehman finished first, winning a total of $1,780,000, and was named the Tour Player of the Year. Corey Pavin played in the same number of tournaments with essentially the same equipment and won $851,000.

Is there a difference between Lehman and Pavin? One earned almost a million dollars more than the other. But what about the difference in their play? Is Lehman really that much better than Pavin?

The PGA keeps track of the average strokes per round for all the tournament players. The final statistics show that in winning his $1,780,000 Tom Lehman averaged 69.71 strokes for every eighteen holes of golf he played on the Tour. Corey Pavin averaged 70.43. That's right! Seventy- two hundredths of a stroke cost Corey Pavin $929,000 in winnings! Seventy-two hundredths of a stroke, the little extra effort, the difference between good and great.

In 1995 Greg Norman was the top money winner on the PGA Tour with an average score of 69.06, earning $1,655,000. Number nine that year was Vijay Singh, averaging 69.92 and earning $1,108,000. Norman earned fifty percent more than Singh while averaging only eighty-six hundredths of a stroke better per round!

In 1995 the Indianapolis 500 was won by Jacques Villeneuve. In one of the closest finishes in Indianapolis history, Villeneuve won by 2.5 seconds after more than three hours of racing. The estimated payoff to Villeneuve, including lap money and endorsements, was ten times that of the driver who finished second. Do you remember who he was? Neither do I.

In three Olympic Winter Games in 1988, 1992 and 1994, the great women's speedskater, Bonnie Blair, won three consecutive gold medals by fifty-six hundredths of a second—combined!

And talk about obscure second-place finishes! Do you remember Mark Spitz, who won seven gold medals in the Munich Olympics in 1972? It was the most outstanding performance by an amateur athlete in the history of the games. Mark Spitz's largest winning margin to gain worldwide acclaim and attention was less than two full seconds. Can you remember any of the swimmers who finished second behind Spitz? Truly the difference between good and great is just a little extra effort.

The famous 1978 Belmont Stakes race between Affirmed and Alydar was so close that it took the steward twenty minutes to determine that Affirmed had won the race—the eleventh horse in history to win racing's Triple Crown. The payoff and the fame difference between those two horses are incalculable. And so it goes throughout every field of endeavor, even in the company where you work.

As you look for winners for your company, and as you seek to establish a winning environment, think about the difference between winners and losers in baseball. A .200 hitter is moved about by managers the way they change their socks. A .300 hitter like Ken Griffey, Jr. is so valuable that when he fights with his manager, you can guess who they fire.

The difference between a .300 hitter and a .200 hitter is one more hit in every ten trips to the plate. If you take the full count, it's one more hit in every sixty pitches. Look for the potential employee with the slight edge of excellence.

There are several excellent books on interviewing potential employees. I won't attempt to override that great body of knowledge in a few short lines, but let me emphasize that the hiring process must be the beginning of a coach winner relationship. The great coaches are those who constantly seek to minimize uncertainty, and that begins in the hiring process in which you establish the field of play.

Many business managers when interviewing a prospective employee have no concept of what it means to set up the field of play. They go through meaningless routines, like going over the new person's resume: "So you worked at Ford Motor Company. "How're they doing?" or "You went to Clayton Valley High School. Did you know Sue Nelson? Class of '70 too, I believe."

How many business managers waste time reading back the resumé to an applicant as if he or she didn't know what was on it, or as if they are trying to catch the person in a lie.

At my company, the field of play interview goes something like this: "Joan, here's what I've got to have done," I begin. "I would expect you as a member of our marketing staff to do whatever you would have to do to get one of our senior staff people in front of a chief executive officer in a closing situation at least once every five working days. And here's how we calculate that. We have in our company what we call 'mean length of time between closing presentations,' and I'm going to show you how to track that. Your first goal would be to go out and get one. I don't know if that would take a week or a month, but you would need to get one. The second goal would be to get the second in less time than it took for the first. Your third goal would be to get the third in less time than the average of the first two. Your fourth goal would be to continue to beat your average."

(This is also the performance formula I use to start new sales people. I have helped other companies adopt variations of this formula. I know of no other field of play that has worked better in getting new salespeople working productively. After explaining what is expected, I tell the sales people I expect them to chart their progress on a chart similar to the one on the following page.)

I tell the applicants what some of the best and worst performances were by other employees; then I ask them if they would perform in the field of play I have outlined.

I make it clear that their performance would be evaluated on how well they performed within the guidelines, not on personality, charm, appearance, sex, race, how they did at Ford Motor Company, or who they knew in high school.

Then I go into more detail on *how* they could get those closing appointments—the number of contacts that would result in at least one opening presentation every day, and how former employees have done, especially the best ones. When I'm finished, the applicants have a clear picture of the field of play, a way to measure their performance, the record book so they know what to shoot for, and a clear understanding of my expectations. At the conclusion of this interview, I assess their past winning behavior, their commitment to our team direction, and their willingness to learn, grow, and be coached. If these criteria match our needs, we have valuable candidates to become team members. That's the way it is in sports, and that's the way it must be in every business.

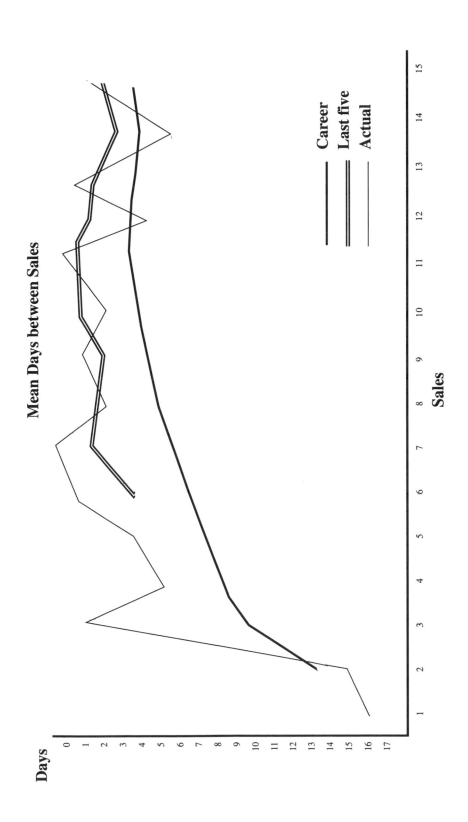

The selection process in sports is based on performance, but it's also based on planned obsolescence, planned over-hiring, and planned preparation for the vagaries of the human animal. Consider that every pro football team carries almost 50 players per team or almost 1,500 players on their league roster, and yet every year they are willing to interview another 438 players who constitute possible candidates for replacement for additional growth in the business. Out of the 438 they're fully prepared to put on the team 50 to 75 new rookies and free agents—fully prepared to replace almost 1/14 of the team. That's about seven percent planned annual turnover. They do not commiserate about injuries or new contracts or competitive offers for other sports or the Canadian football league. They go about overhiring based on their experience with turnover ratio. Recent statistics reveal that 99 percent of all the professional baseball players who have signed a contract since the beginning of the year have never appeared in a major-league game. There is a selection process in nature; there is a process that says that for every Olympic skating champion there are tens of thousands of young aspirants across the country looking for an opportunity to grow. A portion of them make it to the nationals. One of those will become the Katarina Witt or the Peggy Fleming or the Dorothy Hamill of the next Olympiad. Why then do we so often ignore the obvious necessity to over-recruit, over-interview, and over-hire in order to find the very best people we're looking for.

When Tony Dorsett entered the Dallas Cowboys organization, the coach probably said something like this to him: "Tony, here's what we expect from you. You'll be carrying the ball from twenty to thirty-five times a game. We expect you to average close to five yards a carry. We also expect you to decoy and block on this number of plays, and catch so many passes, and sit on the bench when we're doing so and so. Any problem with that?"

Tony might have responded, "Well, in college we didn't do it that way. I don't think I should have to block or catch anything but screenpasses, and I don't want to sit on the bench. Besides, I've talked to one of the other running backs, and I think your expectations are unrealistic."

With a response like that, the coach would probably have

said to Tony, "That's fine. As I see it, you have only one of twenty-seven decisions to make."

"What's that?"

"At which of the other twenty-seven places in the NFL would you like to play next year?"

As you move from hiring to coaching, the commitment to specificity must endure. I am amazed at the number of managers who express dissatisfaction with an employee's performance and then when that hopeful day arrives for the unsatisfactory employee to leave, one of the last things he or she is asked to do is train the replacement. Incredible! The manager abdicates the reins of leadership to someone whose work is unsatisfactory, enabling an undesirable situation to continue.

Managers must recognize that the joy or satisfaction in any experience is measured by the degree to which it meets or exceeds the expectations of the participant. Missed or unfulfilled expectations are the number one cause of relationship failure. It is therefore imperative, from the very beginning, that you form the clearest possible expectations for an employee.

When I say earliest possible moment, I mean the very first day of work, or even earlier, in the recruiting process.

The athlete and the worker are both lost without a clear view of the field of play. Yet, what usually happens when a new employee comes aboard?

We bring them in the first morning and say, "Hi, how are you?" We sit them down at a desk and let another employee, frequently a mediocre performer, describe a sometimes warped picture of the field of play to the new employees.

Typically when you hire new employees you have their undivided attention until the first coffee break. They come in at 8 a.m. in a business suit, calling you Mr. Coonradt, eager to know what they can do for the company. What happens at the coffee break? They meet another employee, someone who's been around a long time and has a confused or warped picture of the field of play.

The new employees come back from the coffee break with the tie undone and the sleeves rolled up, and it's "Chuck, baby. What's cookin'?" Too many managers turn over leadership responsibilities to the wrong people, abdicate the coach's role, and then spend the rest of their supervisory time with employees trying to keep them out of the terminal out-of-bounds area.

My recommendation is that when you hire new people, you don't let them out of your sight for the first forty-eight hours. Have them in all your meetings. Take them to lunch. Don't even let them go to the restroom unless you know they will be alone in there. There's only one chance for a first impression. Make sure new employees get a clear understanding of the correct field of play right from the beginning. It will save a lot of problems later on and could even make the difference between success or failure for an employee.

The need to establish control over new employees and a correct picture right from the beginning is illustrated in what they do to your kid at summer camp. Right off the counselor will invite twelve or fourteen kids onto an open, grassy field to play "kill the counselor." The kids are invited to attack the counselor, all at once, and beat him up—on the surface just a good roughhouse activity. But what happens is that while collectively the kids are wearing down the counselor and will eventually have him pinned to the ground, individually each kid is feeling the counselor's power as he tosses kids here and there during the course of the battle. Each kid is feeling how strong the counselor is.

Four or five days later when one of those kids is goofing off, all the counselor has to do is reach over and grab the kid's arm. If the kid continues to misbehave, the counselor just squeezes a little harder until the kid remembers how easily the counselor tossed him about during the game. He settles down. Subtle, reserved authority is vastly superior to intimidating power.

What many managers don't realize is that how people respond in an organization, and how they assess the organization in their minds, is primarily dependent on their relationship with the person to whom they report. When an employee comes aboard, the manager is in the driver's seat, receiving respect and appropriate responses from the new employee. That respect remains until expectations are not met. It's imperative that expectations be understood and clearly defined.

11

Coaching Winners to Greatness

All coaching is, is taking a player where he can't take himself.

—Bill McCartney,
Retired Head Football Coach
University of Colorado

What is motivation? Drive, incentive, desire, go-power, something you need when you don't have it—like credit at the bank. Billions of dollars are spent on motivation every year. Look at all the pins, plaques, awards, prizes, and, of course, the jackets and blazers—red, blue, white, black, and gold.

What is motivation? If you split this word in half, the first word you have is "motive." And if you add one letter to the back half, you have "action." Motivation is a motive for action—a reason to do something.

Motivation is always present. It may be good, bad, or have no morality at all, but it is always there. It's happening, or not happening, now. It's not something you can buy in a box or bottle and put on a shelf.

There is no such thing as an unmotivated person. Teenagers who are too tired to mow the lawn on a Saturday afternoon are saving energy for a shower and a date! They are motivated, though not in the direction preferred by their parents. Everybody is motivated. Have you had a drink in the last twenty-four hours? You were motivated by thirst to do so. Have you slept in the last twenty-four hours? You were motivated by weariness to do it.

The big question is how to get more motivation in the areas we desire, how to get ourselves and those around us more motivated in business and professional pursuits. In order to know how to get more of it, we must first understand how it works.

There are three kinds of motivation. Fear is the most common form. Parents use it on children, and bosses on workers, all the time. When you have a donkey cart at the bottom of a hill, the fear motivator is the little man cracking the whip. Like most fear motivators, he is sitting down. The theory is simple, but it does not always work, at least not as well as it should. Sometimes the donkey kicks back or sits down. If the hill is steep enough and the load heavy, the donkey gets to a point where he would rather take a beating than continue. People do that too.

Sometimes salespeople get to a point where they would rather sit in the office and starve than get out and work. Most offices have people who are starving to death. The best thing you can do for them is fire them. People are self-determined. You've got to let them do what they want to do. If they want to starve, you can't stop them, but you don't need to pay them while they are doing it.

One of the big problems with fear motivation is that you need somebody with a whip to watch over every donkey. That's expensive. If you have six people sitting around doing the starving routine and you kick one, the other five say, "Yup, see how tough it is." But they still don't go out and do anything. Then the human relations manager will come by and get after you for kicking the person. You can't win with fear.

The next alternative is to use incentive motivation. You get a long stick, tie a carrot on the end, and hold it out in front of the donkey's nose. According to the theory, the donkey will look at the carrot and pull the wagon to the top of the hill. But there are five kinds of situations where the carrot won't work.

One is when the donkey is not hungry enough. Sometimes when you have a donkey that is content with fifteen hundred carrots a month and you put him in a job where he can earn three thousand carrots a month, he'll slow down his performance to catch up with his expectations and needs. He's not hungry.

This happens frequently in the real-estate industry. Take someone who is used to earning $1,200 a month and make him a real estate salesperson. His boss tells him to go out and get a new listing every three days. He does it. Then the boss makes the biggest mistake in the world. He sells a house for the new person, then compounds the mistake by taking the salesperson to the closing and paying him a $3,000 commission in one day. This usually happens his fourth or fifth week in the business. The salesman puts it in his checking account, which is now much bigger than his self-image. He can't get his self-image to go up, so he waits for his checking account to go down.

The second situation where a carrot won't work is when the carrot isn't big enough. The donkey looks ahead at the carrot, then back at the load in the cart, then up at the steepness of the hill, and thinks, "If you think I'm going to pull this load up that hill for one lousy carrot . . ."

The third problem with carrots occurs when the road is too steep. You cannot ask people to do more than they are able. Sometimes taking a class, learning new skills, or gaining more product knowledge will change the situation.

Fourth, carrots won't work when the load is too heavy. This occurs when somebody says, "I know I can make a lot of money in this business, but do you know how many people I have to call on to make a sale?"

The fifth I discovered quite by accident. I was giving a lecture on motivation, and a woman in the back stood up and asked, "Chuck, what do you do if the donkey doesn't like carrots?" As loose as I am, I wasn't prepared for that question. It stopped me dead in my tracks, and I started thinking about it.

It occurred to me that the woman had put me onto one of the fundamental problems of incentive motivation. Not long after that experience I was sitting in the back row at a sales meeting when the vice-president of the company showed the salespeople a beautiful forty-five inch big screen rear projection television. It was to be presented to the top salesperson that month.

I was sitting next to two salespeople who had been around a long time. One of them poked the other and said, "Big deal, it's worth maybe $1,600. If I won, I would have to spend $4,000 to redo the family room just to make the decor right again." The salesperson thought that $1,600 carrot would cost nearly $4,000 to accept. She didn't like the carrot.

Another bad carrot situation occurs when the executive says, "Work hard and we'll make you a manager."

The worker thinks, "Hmmm, manager. That's somebody who works 30 percent longer hours for ten percent less money with three times the heart-attack rate and six times the divorce rate. I don't like your carrot."He'll slow down his performance just short of the prize. If you're going to use carrots, make sure the donkey likes them.

Whereas donkeys may respond best to whips and carrots, people don't. People respond best to their own goals, if they have them. You don't need to treat people like donkeys if you understand goal striving. Reaching goals is a form of winning. People like to win. People who are trying to win by reaching clearly defined goals don't necessarily need carrots or whips. Winning is its own reward.

Remember, there is no such thing as an unmotivated person. Goal setting harnesses that motivation and channels it in the right direction. Through proper goal setting techniques discussed in chapter 2, a person's desire, wants, and needs can be directed into purposeful activity.

The third and most effective form of motivation, self motivation, takes place when people are allowed to choose their own rewards, set their own goals, and decide how they will accomplish those goals. People can be highly motivated in sports because they know nobody is going to change the rules or the boundaries in the middle of the game. Athletes can train and condition with all their heart, knowing that the rules or boundaries are not going to change. In recreation, the rules are clear by which I exchange my talents, abilities, and energy for the things I want to have. Unfortunately, this is frequently not the case in business, and that is why people will pay for the privilege of working harder at play than they will work when they are paid.

Motivation then, the motive for action, is the trade between what I want and what I am willing to give for it.

Consider a balance beam, or a teeter-totter. Keep in mind that motivation is a *motive* for *action*. On the left side you have the weight or intensity of the *motive*. On the right side you have the weight or difficulty of the *action*.

If I offer you a thousand dollars to call me Mr. Coonradt instead of Chuck, you will be motivated to obey, very quickly. A thousand dollars is a strong *motive*, while calling me Mr. Coonradt is an easy *action*. The thousand dollars will quickly motivate you to comply.

If I handed you a quarter in an attempt to get you to run ten miles with a fifty-pound pack on your back, you would think I was crazy. In this case the *action* far outweighs the *motive*, so nothing happens. *The key to motivation is providing motives that outweigh the desired actions.*

The relationship between *motive* and *action* is illustrated perfectly in a holdup that took place in the Old West. A homesteader and his wife were driving their wagon to town when a bandit jumped out of the bushes pointing a six-shooter at them and ordered the man to step down. He obeyed.

"Can you dance?" said the bandit to the man.

"No," responded the frightened farmer.

"We'll see," said the gunman. Then he fired three shots beneath the man's feet. The man danced and the outlaw laughed.

"Can your mule dance?" asked the gunman when the dust had settled.

"No," responded the frightened farmer.

"We'll see," said the gunman. Then he fired three shots beneath the poor animal's feet. The mule reared up and jerked the wagon about, frightening the woman.

The outlaw laughed again, until the woman reached under the seat, pulled out a double-barreled shotgun, and pointed it at the gunman.

"Boy," she said, "Is that a six-shooter in your hand?"

"Yes, ma'am," said the startled outlaw, beginning to wish he were somewhere else, realizing he had fired all six shots.

"Son," she continued, "have you ever kissed a mule?"

"No, ma'am," he said, looking up into the barrel of the shotgun, "but I'm looking forward to the privilege with great anticipation."

Whenever the motive outweighs the action you are going to get results. Everybody in the world has a balance beam in their head. Motivation is simply the process of piling things on the motive side until movement occurs and the action gets off the ground.

The bottom line in motivation is getting the balance beam to move. If you are a fear motivator and nothing is moving, you get a bigger whip. A shotgun at five feet is more effective than a pistol at a thousand yards. The problem is application. You can kick people out of the office, but you can't be with them every minute to make sure they are working. You can't afford a supervisor with a whip to oversee every worker.

If you are an incentive motivator and nothing is happening, you get a bigger carrot. But in a time of shrinking profit margins, you can't really afford bigger and bigger carrots. It would be nice to give everyone a $100,000 a year guarantee with twelve weeks paid vacation, but most companies would go broke offering that big a carrot. And sometimes you run into workers who don't want carrots.

So how do you get more motivation without investing in a bigger whip and more carrots? The key to successful motivation is individual involvement. That means tying the individual goals of your people to the goals of the business. To win at work, you create a methodology where people and the business are closely linked to grow together with common or compatible goals. In order for this to happen, you must recognize the following factors:

1. *WIIFM—What's in it for me?* A vital question all employees have on their mind when coming to work each morning is "What's in it for me?" Anytime people run into a new situation where they're going to be asked to perform, they've got this question: "What's in it for me?" Sometimes the question isn't verbalized because employees don't want the boss to think they are selfish, troublemakers, or bad employees. Still, the question is there, and a smart manager will recognize it.

2. *WSI—Why should I?* Children ask "Why should I?" a lot, at least until they hear the non-answer "Because I said so" so many times that they give up asking. Parents give this non-answer because they don't know or are too lazy to figure out the real answer. They would be better off saying, "I don't know."

When people ask you with their mouth or their eyes (not all questions are asked with the mouth) "Why should I?" or "What's in it for me?" they are attempting to become self-motivated.

They are saying, "Manager, my beam's not tilted yet." "I haven't decided to go." "Help me out." "Let me understand more." "Tell me again." "Motivate me!"

There's something about the way people are put together that makes it almost impossible for them to do something until they understand why. Have you ever been in a situation where somebody asked you to do something new or unexpected without telling you why? Remember how hard it was to do it, if you did it at all?

I was working in the purchasing department of a company once when the president came in and said, "Would you look at the XYZ account?"

"Sure," I said. "What am I looking for?"

"Just look at it," he said.

"Why?" I asked.

"Never mind. I just want you to go through every invoice that we've had from them for the last year."

"What am I looking for?" I repeated.

"I can't tell you. Just look at it."

I admit this is an extreme case, but it really happened. If the manager had said he suspected that somebody was stealing from us or that a purchasing agent was on the take, I could have waded into the project with a purpose. But I didn't know what he wanted. It took me three hours to get sufficiently motivated to go through the file. I did the job because he told me to do it, not because I understood what was to be accomplished. There was little self-motivation to achieve anything. Then when I was finished, he had the nerve to ask me to give him an analysis of what I had found.

There was a new husband who didn't know why his bride cut both ends off the ham as she prepared for their first Easter dinner. He asked her why. She didn't know, only that she had learned it from her mother. Later, when the mother arrived for dinner, the young husband asked her why she and her daughter cut the ends off of ham. The mother answered that she didn't know why, only that she had learned it from her mother, who would soon arrive to share the dinner with them.

When the grandmother didn't know why either, the young husband was so beside himself with curiosity that he got into his car and drove down to the rest home to ask the great-grandmother why she cut both ends off of hams.

The old lady was almost too feeble to speak, but when she finally understood the question, she explained that when she was a little girl, ovens were so small and hams so big that it was usually necessary to cut the ends off in order to get the hams into the oven. Consider all the wasted ham because nobody bothered to ask why.

3. *MMFI—Make me feel important!* A colleague of mine was once doing some industrial research for a manufacturing company where he was trying to measure morale and attitudes. He interviewed people involved in various stages of the manufacturing process. In one area people were gluing what appeared to be pieces of white plastic onto pieces of hardwood, a very tedious and boring task. My friend went up to the first worker and asked, "How do you like your job?"

The man said it was a crummy job.

"What are you doing?" my friend asked.

"I'm putting these white things on these hard blocks."

"How do you like the company?"

"I don't," the man said.

"How do you like the benefits?"

"Who cares? They're not so great."

The researcher got similar responses from the next four or five workers. Then he came to a little old lady with her white hair tied up in a bun. She was whistling. The production charts showed that her production rate was fifty percent above the average.

"How do you like the company?" he asked.

"It's a great place to work," she responded. "Best job I ever had."

"How do you like the benefits?

"They're super."

"How do you like your boss?"

"She's great."

"By the way," asked the interviewer. "What do you do?"

"I make pianos."

What she had figured out was that she was assembling piano keys. She knew that the fingers of a master or the hands of an inquiring child were going to use her keys to bring joy to themselves and others. She felt important about what she was doing, and she was motivated by that feeling of importance.

4. *Different strokes for different folks.* Mao Tse-Tung knew how to motivate people. He went in with a small band of Chinese communists and took control of China away from Chiang Kaishek, who wanted democracy. By our standards Chiang Kaishek was right and had the best interests of the people at heart, but while he preached democracy and freedom, Mao Tse-Tung was promising food, clothing, and shelter—what the people wanted and needed most at the time. Mao won. He had the uncanny ability to match the motives of his followers to the things he wanted accomplished. Great motivators can get a group of people to accomplish a single objective for a variety of individual reasons.

Think about the person in your office who is most in need of motivation. For an eye-opening experience, try filling out the form on the next page. Do you know the person's spouse's name? Do you know the age and primary activities of his or her kids? What hobbies does this person have? How involved is the person in these hobbies? Do you know where this person would like to be in your company in three years? Does your assessment agree with that? Do you know what this person's net worth is and what he or she would like it to be? If you went out of business, what would this person do to make a living?

By now you're probably beginning to feel a little inadequate, and I'm not even halfway through my list of questions. The point I am making is that *nobody can motivate a stranger with consistency.* Your ability to motivate people is directly related to how well you know them and how well you're able to match company goals with their needs and desires. You need to know as much as possible about the people you want to motivate.

And the reverse is true, too. They need to know as much as possible about you, the manager, and the company, too. *Nobody can do what you do unless they know what you know.* You cannot expect people to think the way you think unless they have the information you have.

A typical example is the boss who receives what he considers a bad profit-and-loss statement, gets mad, stuffs it in the drawer

126

Employee Awareness Questionnaire

How well do you know your people? Think of a subordinate or someone with whom you have less than an ideal motivational relationship. How would you answer these questions?

1. Name of employee's spouse or closest relative.

2. Ages and first names of children.

3. What does he/she like to do off the job? List three favorite non-work activities. Do you know his/her level of performance in each of these areas? Do you know about awards or special recognition the person has received?

4. Name one thing each of his/her children is good at.

5. What does he/she think his/her next position in the company will be?

   How soon will he/she be ready to accept it (in his/her mind)?

   How closely does this agree with your assessment?

6. Do you know what he/she would do if the company went out of business?

7. Where does this person like to invest money?

8. What are the person's three greatest fears?

so nobody will see it, and then walks around with a scowl on his face for an entire month, hoping it will be better next time. He walks up to somebody taking an extra three minutes on a coffee break and says, "Don't you understand how much trouble we're in around here?" The employee says, "No." And the boss decides the employee is irresponsible and doesn't care.

If you want to get more self-motivation in people, get to know them better. If someone in your office is worried about getting bread on the table next week, you must know about it. If you've got someone with a $10,000 balloon payment due on a piece of real estate next month, you must know about that too. Know what your people need and let them see that you and your organization offer a way for them to get it. They may not stay with you forever, but they'll perform better while they do.

12

Winning at the Game of Work

Every day, people need to know if they have won or lost.

—Chuck Coonradt

Following are some real examples of companies taking the motivating principles of athletics and applying them in the business world. As you read these examples, think of ways to apply these principles to your own business.

Cash Flow at a Retail Lumber Yard

On one occasion I was called in by a retail lumber company with three locations. The company was about to sell its best piece of real estate in an effort to improve cash flow. It had owned that piece of property for over thirty years, and the transfer fees and taxes would take a huge chunk of the money. They called me in for a "second opinion" before taking the plunge.

Since I believe there is no such thing as a cash flow problem, my initial investigation uncovered what appeared to be a slackening of credit control and, more serious, a loosening up in purchasing controls affecting inventory turnover.

I recommended a twenty-four-month historical review of receivables and inventory. For the receivable measurement, I selected working days of credit sales outstanding and unpaid. This was arrived at as follows:

$$\frac{\text{Last 90 days' credit sales}}{66 \text{ working days}} = \begin{array}{c} \text{Average daily credit} \\ \text{sales outstanding} \end{array}$$

$$\frac{\begin{array}{c}\text{Current period ending} \\ \text{accounts receivable balance}\end{array}}{\begin{array}{c}\text{Average daily} \\ \text{credit sales outstanding}\end{array}} = \begin{array}{c}\text{Working days of} \\ \text{credit sales} \\ \text{uncollected}\end{array}$$

For the inventory we measured the weeks of inventory on hand.

$$\frac{\begin{array}{c}\text{Last 13 weeks sales } \times \\ \text{cost of goods sold percent}\end{array}}{13} = \begin{array}{c}\text{Average weekly cost} \\ \text{of goods sold} \\ \text{in dollars}\end{array}$$

$$\frac{\text{Period ending inventory}}{\begin{array}{c}\text{Average weekly cost of goods sold} \\ \text{in dollars}\end{array}} = \begin{array}{c}\text{Weeks of inventory} \\ \text{on hand}\end{array}$$

These measurements were not very unusual, but they are excellent Results to Resource Ratios.

We found that the working days of credit sales outstanding and unpaid had grown from a low of forty-three days to a high at the present time of sixty-seven days. That increase in twenty-four days of sales outstanding tied up just under a quarter of a million dollars of operating capital.

Our findings in the inventory area were even more remarkable. In a previous year's peak selling time of optimum turnover, the inventory had been reduced to the equivalent of a 8.3 weeks of inventory on hand. No one could recall that there had been any unusual problems in filling orders, no increase in out-of-stock items, no increase in unhappy customers. The inventory, however, had been allowed to grow to 16.7 weeks in stock. The additional seven weeks of inventory tied up an additional $200,000 of operating capital. In just two areas, the introduction of scorekeeping—of keeping historical measurements—uncovered the opportunity to recover almost half a million dollars!

I recommended to management that they hold up on the sale of the real estate and get to work on the receivables and inventory. Thirteen weeks later receivables had been reduced to 53 (from 67) days outstanding, releasing $150,000 in working capital. Eighteen weeks later the inventory level was back to twelve weeks, releasing an additional $100,000 of operating capital. It was no longer necessary to sell the piece of real estate.

Let me emphasize that I am not talking about magic techniques to swamp the lucky executive with fistfuls of cash, though I have witnessed some seemingly miraculous results when proper scorekeeping methods were implemented. What I am talking about is players or competitors gaining an increased awareness of each opportunity to score.

Charting measurements over time, sometimes called a historical review, can magnify the understanding of measurement information many times.

But don't make the mistake of oversimplifying the problem. A golf course may be seventy-two hundred yards long with a par of seventy-two strokes. You may score par by averaging a hundred yards per stroke. The hundred-yard drives are a cinch, but what about the hundred-yard putts? Only by accurate scorekeeping and measurement of every part of the game do you improve each part of the game and come out a winner. Your drives will go well over one hundred yards, and your putts will never get close to the hundred-yard mark, but as you keep score on each part of the game, your averages will improve. The same principle applies in business.

Increased Profitability for a Communications Firm

Sometimes it's important to spend time getting the rules straight before starting to play. I was once involved in such an opportunity. A public communications company called me in to help with budget plans for the new year. The firm had been languishing for years in a rather flat but still acceptable profit picture. Their operating profit had been bouncing between $1.4 and $1.9 million a year for four years. In the most recent year, it had dropped to $1.7 million.

It was September, and the chief executive called me in to see if I could help get their fall budget and planning session off to a better start.

In our preliminary discussions, the chief executive discussed what the experts were saying about the stock market, what he thought were the plans of the competition for the coming year, the relationship with the holding company, and a dozen other irrelevant items used in previous years to get the budgeting process underway. It became clear to me that we needed to clarify the rules before the game began.

I asked the chief executive what kind of profit picture he would like for the new year. He responded by saying that the best they had ever done was $2.25 million.

"Would you like that again next year?" I asked.

"I don't know," he said. "I haven't finished studying all the economic predictions." He also indicated a string of unprofitable Januarys due to the fact that the budgeting for the new year, which was started in September, was never finished by January.

"Would you like to earn that much?" I persisted, realizing that his own will was among the most important factors in that company's profit planning.

"Yes," he finally said. "I believe I'd like to take a shot at it." And so we outlined a $2.25 million operating plan.

"What percentage of your profit comes from your major operating division?" I asked, and he said 86 percent had been the traditional contribution of the major division. We assigned 86 percent of the profit to the flagship division.

"Is that fair?" he asked.

"Do you believe it is?" I responded.

"I do," he said.

The next division accounted for just under 10 percent, so we rounded its share up to 10 percent, and the third division accounted for 4 percent. We allocated 100 percent of the corporate profit goal based on the historical percentage of revenue contribution. The president then mentioned all the other areas of responsibility that consumed various amounts of his budget. We agreed after a brief discussion that those areas would be subordinated to the three profit-making divisions and would not be discussed further until the plans for the profit-producing divisions had been established.

Safely convinced in my own mind that he and I were in accord, I left him that Friday afternoon looking forward to a Monday morning group meeting with the division heads.

At the Monday meeting he said, "Gentlemen, I've prepared the budget, and I'm going to ask you to meet some very simple requirements."

He then presented each of the division heads with an envelope containing the total net dollars of operating profit expected from each person. After the initial yelling and screaming subsided, the managers went back to their offices and in half the normal time prepared operating plans that would get the chief executive officer the amount of profit he asked for. The operating plans were finished by Thanksgiving, whereas in previous years they had not been finished before the end of the year. Though that initial meeting was tense, it was as it should have been, the chief executive communicating clearly with his top lieutenants, telling them exactly what he expected them to do.

The company did not achieve the $2.25 million goal that year. It achieved $3.4 million, due mostly to two things. One, the early completion of the operating plans enabled the divisions to be off and running by the first of the year, whereas in previous years the plans hadn't been agreed upon until the end of January. Two, the general manager of the flagship division began to strum the strings of his imagination and created one of the greatest incentive purchase programs in that company's history. He said he knew what he had to do, and because of that he went way past the budget. That year the meetings focused on profit and growth rather than on the usual nitpicking about expenses. With the profit goals clearly established at the outset, many of the negative, unnecessary activities were pushed aside. The lieutenants loved the new system. They had clearly defined goals and a way to win. The leadership had come from the top. It was specific, direct, and intense.

The chief executive later confessed to me that he didn't sleep well the Sunday night before that meeting, and that the entire weekend had been one of the most miserable of his entire life. As we laughed about it fifteen months later over a record profit-and-loss statement, he told me that his profit goal for the coming year was $4.4 million. He had previously rejected my suggestion of a minimum 15 percent annual increase in profit dollars as being too tough and unrealistic.

Improving Maintenance for a Trucking Firm

One time I was called into a $10 million a year trucking company to work on maintenance problems. First, we measured maintenance costs (labor and parts) as a percentage of total billings. Although this measurement was nearly twice the national average for similar firms, the measurements didn't show any dramatic fluctuations, so they were not very useful. We did not have anything to compare the measurements against.

So we devised a nonstandard measurement—the average miles between breakdowns. We borrowed this idea from the U.S. Defense Department, which for years has been measuring the time between failures of its defense systems. We did the same thing with the trucks.

It was a self-administered scorekeeping system with the mechanics taking readings from the odometers of each truck when there was a breakdown. Routine maintenance and servicing were not included.

The mechanics or the supervisors of maintenance in each of the garage facilities built their own scorecard for each vehicle in their care. It was very simple, not cumbersome at all. The person in charge would simply subtract the odometer reading from the reading at the previous breakdown to get the miles between breakdowns.

Once the system was operational, we discovered one service

terminal that needed immediate attention—its trucks were averaging only 750 miles between breakdowns. For the first time the company had an accurate record of how the various repair facilities were doing in comparison to each other. The system also enabled us to compare the service records of trucks from different manufacturers. We could also compare parts performance—spark plugs, axles, tires, and so on.

As a result of the new miles-between-breakdown measurement, the company increased the rotation frequency of vehicles and reduced overall transportation repair costs by 1.2 percent of sales. In that $10 million company, that resulted in an annual savings of $125,000.

Improving the Customer's Opportunity to Give You Money

I was called in to consult with a company that built custom overhead cranes for materials handling. As I began the investigation, I took a look at receivables, as I always do. Although receivables are normally updated monthly, they must be watched daily.

The standard way to track receivables is an aging report—dividing the money owed you into thirty-, sixty-, and ninety-day blocks. The aging report shows what percentage of the money owed you falls into each of the categories. When you confront the average collections manager on the status of receivables, he or she will give you some evasive rhetoric about percentage—that it is up two percent or down two percent, and that the total amount over ninety days is X. Good information, but you don't know where you are headed. You don't know if the situation is really getting better or worse.

The first measurement I added for the crane company was the number of days of business outstanding—the amount of business done in the last ninety days that they had not been paid for. This measurement is concise, flexible, and easily measured, and it gives rapid feedback. It tells you how good you are at getting the money owed you and if you are getting better or worse at collecting it.

As we began to track the number of days of business outstanding, we quickly recognized the company had a real problem with receivables. The number of days of business outstanding was approaching ninety.

As we began to discuss how the problem might be corrected, a casual slip of the tongue caught my immediate attention. Someone said, "I'll bet if we could get our invoices out faster, we'd get paid better."

"Tell me more," I said. "How long does it take now?"

What I heard was altogether too typical, an observation management response—a lot of talk about one invoice here, another there, two that had this or that problem. People involved in management by observation always cite the examples that reinforce their personal point of view. It was evident that nobody really knew how soon the invoices were sent out. No measurement existed.

I set up a simple scorecard to be completed by the invoice clerk under the direction of the controller. They began to identify and track the number of days required from job completion date until the invoice was in the mail to the customer.

On the first batch of twenty invoices, the average processing time was thirteen working days. The process of checking against the bid, auditing, price checking, and double checking was causing a full month's delay in the customer's opportunity to pay.

Of course, the customer is never eager to pay, regardless of when the bill comes. But we decided the money would come faster if the invoices were sent out sooner, closer to the work completion dates. We also reasoned that most of the customers paid in some kind of billing cycle and that if we could get invoices to them sooner, we'd increase our chances of catching an earlier cycle.

The scorecard told us the invoicing performance was not up to our expectations. Armed with that information the controller began to explore the causes of the slow invoicing and how the situation might be corrected. Using additional scorecarding, he began to study the invoicing process, uncovering the bottlenecks. One by one he identified the problem areas and began to snip away at them. Within six weeks the average number of working days to produce an invoice to the customer had gone from thirteen down to three. We had eliminated almost two weeks out of the time required to get the invoice to the customer. Within six weeks we saw a noticeable improvement in collections.

Controlling Seasonal Unprofitability in a Bottling Company

Another great example of using scorekeeping to bring seasonal fluctuations under control occurred in a small bottling company. They retained my services during a marginal profit year in an effort to curtail losses after the first of the year. The company traditionally had strong sales and profitability during the summer and fall months, peaking at the holiday season. After the first of the year, however, the company always entered a period of thirty to ninety days in the red.

In selecting a Results to Resource Ratio, we identified two items that did not fluctuate with inflation: costs or economy. The sales manager began to track each route or truck on the basis of cases delivered per gallon of fuel consumed by the truck. Adjustments were made for propane and diesel vehicles, and also for flatbed and gooseneck trailers. Almost immediately there was an increase for the first time in its history, the company operated in the black during January and February. When management saw this working, they introduced a cases per mile scorecard for their routes that enabled them to decrease labor costs in accordance with seasonal drops in sales. This one measurement alone enabled the company to reduce delivery costs by 15 percent with no appreciable decrease in sales revenues.

Shifting the Emphasis from People to Dollars for the March of Dimes

One of my clients was the volunteer supervisor of a March of Dimes telethon. The most money the group had ever raised was $78,000. In the past the goals of the person in charge had been measured in number of people contacted and other activities related to the fund-raising process.

We implemented a new program in which the emphasis was shifted from people contacted to dollars raised. We set up a tracking system based on performance in past years. The measurement system had the ability to update the progress hourly during the telethon.

With the new system in place, a goal of $100,000 was set, $22,000 higher than any amount previously raised. That first year they raised $110,000. Within three years the telethon was raising more than $200,000 a year.

Even Waste Can Be Measured

A fencing company asked me to help improve its overall productivity. The first thing we did was set up a noninflationary measurement for the entire company. We charted pounds of product per person-hour. We included management and clerical employees as well as production workers in the measurement. We started out at 127 pounds per person-hour, and after four months productivity had increased to 196 pounds per person-hour.

As we implemented the tracking system, it was necessary to devise several intermediate scorecards. One of the greatest challenges was keeping track of the scrap produced when six- and eight-gauge galvanized wire was drawn into nine- and eleven-gauge wire to be made into basket-weave fencing. The supervisor in charge of this drawing operation had no idea whether he was winning or losing. His goal seemed to be to minimize losses in a situation where dies would wear out and the gauge was inconsistent most of the time. Very little was ever right about the operation. When the operation was at peak performance, two nine-cubic-yard dumpsters were filled daily with scrap from broken dies, broken runs, operator error, and variety of other causes. The president of the organization was well aware that the company was spending thousands of dollars a month in hauling costs alone to dispose of the scrap wire.

At the suggestion of one of my associates, the company installed a device to weigh the scrap and provide immediate feedback to the operator. It was soon discovered that some of the operators were more wasteful than others, that some were not suited for that particular job. These were transferred or fired. Within six weeks of the installation of the weighing device, the amount of scrap had been reduced from two bins a day to two bins a week, an almost 80 percent reduction. Thus, there was an increased amount of wire going into finished galvanized fencing. The scrap disposal costs were cut by $40,000 a year.

A Simple Measurement to Reduce Shelf-Stocking Costs

Cases per person-hour has been a good item to track in distributor warehouses and retail stores, particularly grocery stores. I convinced the assistant manager of a small closely held grocery chain to track every delivery over a period of weeks. Productivity ranged from a low of thirty-four cases per person-hour to a high of over sixty cases per person-hour. We recognized immediately that the workers' goals had never been expressed in productivity but rather in survival until the end of the shift. We could see that in filling the schedule, fifteen-hundred-case loads were being done in thirty person-hours at a rate of over fifty cases per person-hour. Several days later a thousand-case load delivered to the same store would require the same number of person-hours— evidence that Dr. Parkinson's laws were indeed at work.

As the crews became aware they were being tracked, productivity picked up. The crews were allowed to go home when the work was finished. And management amply determined that they could pay the crew on a piece-rate basis, which allowed more flexibility in scheduling. Once that was firmly in place, shelf-stocking costs dropped by 27 percent.

An Ideal Tracking System for New Salespeople

Once I was contacted by a new independent sales agent who

was not meeting his sales goals, not even coming close to his expectations. As we discussed the problem, our attention focused on two ideas. One was that if we asked new salespeople to sell one contract their first month and two their second month, we were telling them that they had to double their productivity in one month—their first month, the hardest month of their career. That was no good.

The other idea we kept talking about was something I recalled from a purchasing class in college about a government specification on weapon systems called "mean time between failures." We synthesized the two ideas into what we called MDBS (mean days between sales). We created the following preliminary goals program for new salespeople.

1. Get your first sale as quickly as you can, wherever you can, from whomever you can, for whatever price you can. (We even considered taking a lower price in an effort to give the new salesperson a good closing experience as soon as possible.)

2. Get your second sale in less time than you got the first one.

3. Get your third sale in less than the average of the first two.

4. Continue to beat your average.

After a dismal first ninety days when he was on the verge of resignation, this young man implemented the MDBS tracking system. At the end of a year he was recognized by his company as the national rookie of the year.

This MDBS formula has worked better than any other start-up goal setting process I know of, and it is getting more people into solid sales production in more areas of the country than anything else I know.

The MDBS enables the sales manager to coach salespeople individually. It gives new salespeople a chance to feel the excitement of success through gradual improvement in their production.

In Conclusion

The principles in this book improved performance and increased profitability in nearly every imaginable type of business or organization. These principles are timeless. They work as well in business as they do in athletics and recreation.

Once people are sold on the value of scorekeeping and their personal goals are consistent with the overall goals of the company, the rules are clearly defined, and Results to Resource Ratios are in place, allowing the people to know if they are winning or losing every day, their increased productivity will be phenomenal. Being sold is the key, and choice makes the difference. When players help develop their own scorekeeping system, they own it, care for it, and fight to retain it.

When the principles in this book are applied in the workplace, workers will give the same enthusiasm and energy to their work that they give to their recreation. They will enjoy work as much as they enjoy play. And they will learn how to win at the game of work.

To obtain additional copies of *The Game of Work*, visit your local bookstore, Amazon.com, or call toll-free 1-800-438-6074.

The Game of Work, Inc. is dedicated to helping you implement the principles in this book. They can provide a live presentation of those principles to your company or group, as well as, in-house implementation of the concepts with your management team. For further information contact:

The Game of Work, Inc.
1912 Sidewinder Drive, Suite 201
Park City, UT 84060
(801) 645-9666
Toll Free: (800) 438-6074
email: game@gameofwork.com

A condensed version of *The Game of Work* on cassette tape is available from The Game of Work, Inc.

Index

What Is the Game of Work?

The Game of Work is an action-packed seminar to provide you with the keys to enjoying work as much as play.

The Game of Work examines the phenomenon that people often work harder at sports and athletic endeavors than they do at their jobs. Why? Because in sports, a participant has constant feedback on how he or she is doing—the score is known and the effort necessary to win is established. In work, feedback is often unreliable, inconsistent, or nonexistent. The participant seldom knows the score or what it takes to win.

Chuck Coonradt is a graduate of Michigan State University and did his graduate studies at UCLA. He is an internationally recognized consultant and lecturer in the field of goal setting and profit improvement.

As author of *The Game of Work*, Chuck Coonradt takes the winning techniques of recreation and applies them to the workplace to increase profitability and productivity. A small sampling of clients who have implemented *The Game of Work* include the Quaker Oats Company, Pepsi-Cola Company, Dow Chemical, Fleming Companies Inc., American Stores Company, General Foods Corporation, United Artists Cablesystem Corporation, Young Electric Sign Company, Martin Door Manufacturing, Wendy's, Resource Net International, Columbia HCN, Pacificare, Hoechst Celanese, and Browning-Ferris Industries.

What You Can Expect to Learn

- *A fresh look at motivation and scorekeeping through:* attitudes of winners—choices— observation—judgments—scorekeeping—implementing a system—turning measurement into a benefit—setting criteria for goals
- *Motivation:* self-evaluation—feedback—types of motivation—coaching
- *Feedback:* graphs and charts—rules and mechanics of scorecards—guidelines for effective feedback

- *Areas of control:* the power of the Results to Resources Ratio as a scorekeeping tool
- *How to set up a Results to Resources scorekeeping system*
- *Goal setting and motivation*
- *Personal goal-setting*
- *Understanding the field of play*
- *Learning how to win every day!*

Professional Services

- Speeches (two-hour, four-hour, or full-day)
- Workshops for your personnel, customers, associations, company meetings, and so on
- Implementation—a fully customized program of five half-days of specific *Game of Work* implementation with *guaranteed results*
- Ski & Scheme—3 day executive ski retreat at Deer Valley Resort

For additional information, call:
1-800-438-6074

or write:
The Game of Work
1912 Sidewinder Drive, Suite 201
Park City, Utah 84060
www.gameofwork.com
Fax: (801) 649-2928
email: game@gameofwork.com